CALL  D

*A Theology of Vocation
and
Lifelong Commitment*

Marie Theresa Coombs, Hermit
and
Francis Kelly Nemeck, O.M.I.

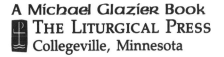
A Michael Glazier Book
THE LITURGICAL PRESS
Collegeville, Minnesota

A Michael Glazier Book published by The Liturgical Press

Cover design by Fred Petters

1	2	3	4	5	6	7	8	9

Library of Congress Cataloging-in-Publication Data

Coombs, Marie Theresa.
    Called by God : a theology of vocation and lifelong commitment /
Marie Theresa Coombs and Francis Kelly Nemeck.
        p.   cm.
    "A Michael Glazier Book."
    ISBN 0-8146-5909-8
    1. Vocation. 2. Vocation, Ecclesiastical.   I. Nemeck, Francis
Kelly, 1936– . II. Title.
    BX2380.C644 1992
    248.4—dc20   92-18817
                                                        CIP

To
Christ Jesus,
The Wisdom of God

in
Heartfelt Appreciation
of
Gerald Coombs

Now your life is hidden with Christ in God.
When Christ, our life, is revealed,
*   you too will be revealed with him in glory* (Col 3:3-4).

Contents

Abbreviations   vi

Introduction   1

God's Willing

1. The Will of God   9
2. God's Willing, God's Calling, God's Caring   19
3. The Will of God and Vocation   29

God's Calling

4. Chosen by God   39
5. Called by God   49
6. Consecrated by God   56
7. Consecrated unto God   63

God's Developing Call

8. Christian Vocational Lifestyles   73
9. Dawning Light   82
10. Pilgrimage into the Unknown   91
11. Developmental Patterns Consciousness   99

Lifelong Commitment to God's Developing Call

12. Vocational Commitment   115
13. Pastoral Implications Related to Lifelong Commitments   121
14. The Responsibility of the Christian Community in Vocational Awakening   133
15. The Sound of Gentle Silence   141

Conclusion: Vocation as Mystery   151

Abbreviations

Contemplation   Francis Kelly Nemeck and Marie Theresa Coombs, *Contemplation*, Liturgical Press, 1982 (write The Liturgical Press, St. John's Abbey, Collegeville, MN 56321-7500; phone 612-363-2213; fax 612-363-3299).

O Blessed Night   Francis Kelly Nemeck and Marie Theresa Coombs, *O Blessed Night: Recovering from Addiction, Codependency and Attachment based on the insights of St. John of the Cross and Pierre Teilhard de Chardin*, Alba House, 1991 (write Alba House, 2187 Victory Boulevard, Staten Island, NY 10314-6603; phone 1-800-343-2522).

Receptivity   Francis Kelly Nemeck, *Receptivity*, Vantage Press, New York, N.Y., 1985 (out of print).

Spiritual Direction   Francis Kelly Nemeck and Marie Theresa Coombs, *The Way of Spiritual Direction*, Liturgical Press, 1985.

Spiritual Journey   Francis Kelly Nemeck and Marie Theresa Coombs, *The Spiritual Journey: Critical Thresholds and Stages of Adult Spiritual Genesis*, Liturgical Press, 1987.

TDNT   Gerhard Kittel and Gerhard Friedrich, eds., *Theological Dictionary of the New Testament*, I–X, Eerdmans, 1964–1977.

TDOT   Johannes Botterweck and Helmer Ringgren, eds., *Theological Dictionary of the Old Testament*, I–VI, Eerdmans, 1974–1991.

Introduction

As children, relatives would sometimes ask us: "What are you going to be when you grow up?" "What do you want to do?" Without reflecting very much on the significance of their questions, they were already inquiring into our vocational awareness at a very early age.

During adolescence we went on to make specific choices which marked the beginning of a direction toward the future. Throughout adulthood we have been engaged in forming and living out certain commitments with regard to personal relationships, meaningful lifestyles and chosen professions or careers.

The ability to make those decisions and to sustain those commitments is not, however, merely the fruit of emotional and psychological maturation. As Christians, we believe that our choices and commitments have also a transcendent quality. They are related to a God-given destiny and, hence, are profoundly imbued with a faith dimension. Although we may not advert to the fact until much later in life, the decisions which correspond to our deepest longings proceed from a developing sense of vocation.

In terms of its ultimate realization, the goal of that vocation is transformation in God, by God—our personal deification. Vatican II touched on that truth under the heading "Universal Call to Holiness."[1]

---

[1]"Dogmatic Constitution on the Church," *The Documents of Vatican II*, 39–42. See *Contemplation*, 13–20.

In terms of what is taking place this side of the resurrection, we are in the process of returning to the Father with Christ in the Spirit. At the core of that pilgrimage is our personal calling—an individual vocation flowing out of the universal call to holiness.[2]

Because each of us is a unique person, each of us is on a unique journey. From the instant of our individual creation, God implants a spiritualizing direction within our inmost being. In so doing, the Lord consecrates us. That spiritual directedness develops into "a fire burning in [our] heart, imprisoned in [our] bones. [We] cannot resist it for very long" (Jer 20:9). We belong to the Lord from the outset, and we are destined to be completely God's in the end.

When we use the term "vocation," we do not ordinarily advert to just how comprehensive that word is. In effect, it refers to three distinguishable callings—or, to put it more accurately, three interrelated aspects of a single complex mystery. They are:

- *who* the Lord calls us to be;
- *how* the Lord calls us to become ourselves in God;
- *what* the Lord calls us to do for God and for others.

The first refers to self-identity, the second to vocational lifestyle and the third to mission or ministry.

Who. We are called to be fully ourselves in God. Ultimately, that means becoming whole persons deified in Father, Son and Spirit; totally realized individuals transformed in God by participation.[3] In this life, we never know completely who we are. Our deepest self remains a mystery. Yet, as faith intensifies, we receive increasing insight into this "who" of ours. By means of a certain "comprehensive wisdom and spiritual understanding" (Col 1:9), we grow in self-knowledge. That vague though impelling self-awareness flows primarily from a gradual, loving and intuitive experience of ourselves rather than from analytical, deductive and scientific reasoning.

How. There are many "how's" on our spiritual journey: the various aspects of discipleship (John 8:31; 13:35), the exercise of the corporal works of mercy (Matt 25:34-40), the implementa-

[2] See *Spiritual Direction,* 15–32; *Spiritual Journey,* 40–52.
[3] See *Contemplation,* 16–18; *Spiritual Journey,* 19–21, 42–52.

tion of the gifts of the Spirit (Gal 5:22), etc. Each of them contributes to how the Lord deifies us. Yet, there is a special "how" which serves as an all-embracing milieu for the others: our vocational lifestyle. God calls us to personal divinization in the context of a certain way of life. Some lifestyles are mutually exclusive, for example: married, single, celibate. Others coexist. For instance, the apostolic life can coexist with any of the above.

What. God brings everyone into this life to do something, to accomplish some mission, to make a positive contribution to the Body of Christ. Even a stillborn child can have a lifelong impact on the parents. For many Christians, several missions coexist, as for example: administrator-educator-parent; priest-pastor-chaplain. For other people, a number of ministries or careers succeed one another, for instance: teacher, nurse, missionary. The possible combinations of apostolates to which God commissions us are myriad.

Vocationally speaking, who we are, how we are becoming and what we are sent to do initiate with God and redound to God. The fact that any one of us exists at all is not merely accidental. That our lifestyle is such and such is not purely arbitrary. That we are involved in a certain mission is not simply by chance. The Lord chooses us to be unique persons, to become ourselves in a certain manner and to bear fruit, fruit that will last (John 15:16).

The more we mature, the more the various aspects of our vocation interconnect. Ordinarily, we cannot be our true self in the Lord until we become that person in the way that God wills and until we do what God desires. In a sense, our lifestyle is the matrix of our evolving self-identity, while our ministry is an especially providential means to the fullness of the other two.

We could compare the interrelatedness of the three aspects of the mystery we name "vocation" to the interaction of our right brain, left brain and central nervous system; or again to the interdependence of our lungs, heart and circulatory system. Each organ functions as an integral part of an extremely complex whole. Yet, we can and sometimes must single out one organ for careful examination.

Regarding the three interrelated aspects of calling, our principle focus in this work is Christian lifestyle—our vocational "how." That aspect of vocation refers to the God-given and all-embracing context in which we live and mature in every respect: emotional, intellectual, social, affective, spiritual, etc.

Christians the world over are in search of a vibrant sense of vocation. They seek in faith to understand more what it means to be personally called by God. In this book, we offer a theology of vocation and of lifelong commitment which some people may find new and provocative. We hope that all find it fresh and stimulating.

Our underlying perspective is evolutionary and relational. Not only does the consciousness of our vocation develop as we mature, but also the calling itself evolves throughout a lifetime. Moreover, the development of both our vocation and our vocational awareness evolves relationally; that is, in intimate relatedness with ourselves as maturing individuals, with others as they influence us and with God as the abiding presence of Father, Son and Spirit intensifies within us.

We proceed, first, with a reexamination of the mystery of divine will as it relates to vocational lifestyles. Second, we reflect on the rich biblical data concerning chosen, called and consecrated. Third, we discuss from various points of view the development of vocation and of vocational consciousness leading up to possible lifelong commitment. Fourth, we address choice of vocational lifestyle and commitment thereto as well as their evolution for the remainder of our mortal existence. Finally, we conclude with some thoughts on vocation specifically as mystery.

Our underlying purpose is not only to offer fresh insights, but above all to afford life-giving directions for pilgrims as they sort through the perplexities of vocational discernment. Our primary objective in this book is to establish a theological basis upon which principles for vocational discernment can rest.

Our way of approaching the mystery of vocation in general and the discernment of vocational lifestyles and lifelong commitment in particular is intentionally more reflective than polemic, more inductive than deductive. We do address several thorny issues and pose some difficult questions. Yet, our overriding concern is to suggest possible responses and avenues of resolution. Our theology is reasonable as well as challenging, but above all it is faith-imbued and tested in the crucible of faith experience.

* * *

1. All translations from Hebrew, Greek, Latin, French and Spanish sources—including biblical—are our own. Ordinarily, we adapt these texts to reflect contemporary inclusive language.

2. We deeply respect the need for inclusive language in theological discourse. Yet, contemporary English poses many problems in this regard. To strike a balance between those two factors, we follow these guidelines:

A. When employing singular pronouns to refer to the human person, we always use s/he or him/her.

B. Although grammatically the nouns "God" and "Lord" are masculine in gender, we readily acknowledge the feminine dimension of God and the legitimacy of referring to God as "Mother." To avoid using the masculine pronoun alone, however, we ordinarily repeat the noun.

C. Regarding "Father," especially in biblical texts, we sometimes use the masculine pronoun when repetition of the noun would be cumbersome.

D. Regarding Jesus, we employ the masculine pronoun in reference to him. We do the same with respect to the titles "Christ," "Son" and "Lord" when referring specifically to him.

E. Regarding the Holy Spirit, we usually avoid any pronoun and repeat the noun.

GOD'S WILLING

CHAPTER 1

The Will of God

It would be unthinkable to discuss theologically the mystery of vocation, vocational discernment and lifelong commitment without first broaching the mystery of God's will. Who, how and what the Lord intends for us sets the direction in which we become our true selves and cooperate with God's transforming activity in us and all around us.

We find the complexities of our own will—with its motivations and subterfuges, its compulsions and drives, its likes and dislikes—impossible enough to unravel. But to attempt to delve into the will of God utterly boggles the imagination by comparison:

> Oh, the depths of the riches and the wisdom of God!
> How inscrutable the Lord's judgments!
> How unsearchable God's ways!
> Who has ever penetrated the mind of the Lord? (Rom 11:33-34).

Nonetheless, our faith experience urges us to seek some understanding of this mystery. Not only do we aspire to know God's will, but also the Lord desires us to know something of the divine will so that we can more intentionally and lovingly acquiesce to it. The author of Colossians prayed for that insight:

> In all wisdom and spiritual understanding,
>   may you be imbued with an vibrant knowledge of God's will,
>   so that you may live a life worthy of the Lord,

pleasing God in every way, bearing fruit in every good work
and growing in your experience of the Lord (Col 1:9-10).

Two questions concerning this mystery pose themselves
from the outset: How does God will? And what does God will?
The first question is theoretical and utterly impossible to answer.
It pertains to the inner life of the Trinity. The second, being practical, attains the very core of our personal salvation history. It
requires of us "listening and doing" (Matt 7:24), searching and
responding. Jesus insists: "Whoever puts my Father's will into
practice is my brother and sister and mother" (Matt 12:50).

A. We See as Through a Glass Darkly (1 Cor 13:12)

The fact that we can think and speak of God only by way of
analogy remains a formidable limitation in discussing the mystery of the divine will. At best, we conceive of the Lord in simili-
tudes. Moreover, in every analogy there exists greater dissimili-
tude than sameness. Whatever we say of God—"one," "loving,"
"free," etc.—expresses some truth. But in reality, the Lord infinitely transcends whatever we understand that truth to be.

One of the most common analogical modes of imaging God
is anthropomorphism. That is, thinking and speaking as if the
Lord were human.

What does it mean for us to will? When we "will," we set our
hearts on something that we judge to be of value, and we direct
our energy toward its attainment. Often, we want what we want
when we want it. Our will can be strong, deliberate or precise. It
can also be neutral, arbitrary or vague. Sometimes we want specific things done in a particular way; at other times we have only
a general objective in mind without caring how it is accomplished. A great many people consider it better to be more decisive than openended, more clear than ambiguous, more specific
than generic.

Having some idea of what it means for us to will and having
definite preferences as to what is "better," many persons apply
those judgments and characteristics to the Lord's will. They
would say, therefore, that the divine will is immutable, absolute,
uniform and rigorously determined. It is against this backdrop
that the following classical formula is ordinarily understood:

- God wills good directly.
- God wills physical evil only indirectly.
- God merely permits moral evil.

That idea of the divine will is also the context in which most people think of predestination, foreknowledge and providence.

But must it necessarily be so? Is there not another more dynamic approach to the mystery of God's will? In place of a static absolutist view of the divine will, we propose an evolutionary[1] and relational perspective. This viewpoint is of paramount importance to understanding our theology of vocation, vocational discernment and lifelong commitment.

Yet, no matter how dynamic a theology of the divine will is, our faith-understanding remains sorely limited by created modes of conceptualization and expression. As much as we may prefer otherwise, we continue to think and to talk of God only analogically and in many instances rather anthropomorphically. No matter how insightful our observations, we still see at best "through a glass darkly" (1 Cor 13:12).[2]

B. The Crux of the Question

Every true pilgrim appreciates to some extent that God is unfathomably immanent and at the same time utterly transcendent.

The immanence of God is convincingly stressed in the Bible: for instance, in the Yahwistic tradition and ultimately in the mystery of the incarnation—when God's own "Word became flesh and pitched his tent in our midst" (John 1:14).

The transcendence of God is also evident throughout Scripture. The recurring theology of the Lord's holiness reaches a certain apex in the prophets; for example, in the thrice holy

[1]With Pierre Teilhard de Chardin, we believe that spiritual theology, like all other areas of human searching, has to be re-presented in light of evolution—or, to put it more precisely, in the light of Christogenesis: "Is evolution a theory, a system or a hypothesis? It is all three and more. It is a general condition to which all theories, all systems, all hypotheses must bow and which they must henceforth satisfy if they are to be thinkable and true. Evolution is a light illuminating all facts, a curve that all lines must follow." *Phenomenon of Man* (New York: Harper Torchbooks, 1961) 218.

[2]Literally, St. Paul wrote "through a mirror in an enigma."

revelation of Yahweh in Isaiah 6:3 and in Hosea's association of holiness with God's faithful love. The New Testament proclaims each person of the Trinity "holy."[3]

Intimately associated with divine transcendence are the two interrelated notions of absoluteness and self-sufficiency. To be absolute means to be free from all restriction or restraint, to be independent of anything arbitrary. Self-sufficiency denotes self-containment, freedom from every contingency.

The crux of the question of the divine will, once again, is this: How—from an evolutionary and relational perspective—can we preserve intact God's utter transcendence and absolute self-sufficiency, while at the same time experiencing more deeply God's immanence in terms of receptivity, relativity and responsiveness to the unfolding human situation?

What we term "the divine will" is the meeting point, so to speak, of God's transcendence and God's immanence in our personal lives. The Lord's immanence is itself transcendent. Indeed, God is more intimate to us than we are even to ourselves. Moreover, the Lord's transcendence is also immanent. Both are dynamic, not static.

C. A Trinitarian Perspective

A traditional analogy describing the inner life of the Trinity may shed light on our discussion of the divine will. To describe the processions of the divine persons within the Trinity, patristic and medieval theology use the example of the interrelatedness of knowing and loving within the human person.

The doctrinal postulation states: The Son proceeds from the Father, and the Spirit proceeds from the Father and the Son. Applying the analogy of human knowing and loving to the processions within the Trinity, the scholastics express themselves this way: The Father knowing himself from all eternity generates the Word, his Son. The Father and the Son loving each other from all eternity spirate the Holy Spirit.[4]

From that perspective, the person of the Holy Spirit enjoys a special association with the affective dimension of the Trinity's

---

[3]See *Contemplation*, 14–16.
[4]See *Spiritual Direction*, 16–20.

inner life. Loving is the principal function of willing, as we understand it. By appropriation, therefore, the Holy Spirit enjoys a special association with God's loving/willing rapport with creation.

What might the above analogy and theology be telling us?

Within the Trinity and with regard to God's loving/willing rapport with creation, the theology presented above views the Holy Spirit as transcendently relational, wholly dynamic and extremely elusive. If those attributes are true of the Holy Spirit, they would also seem to be fundamental qualities of God's will.

Thus, because the divine will is transcendently relational, it can somehow be interrelated with our use or abuse of freedom. Because the Lord's will is immanently dynamic, it can have a certain relativity vis-à-vis ours. Because God's will is mysteriously elusive, it may be considerably more general than many people think.

We stress these qualities in contradistinction to, but not necessarily in contradiction with, certain classical conceptualizations of the divine will; namely, immutable, absolute and specific.

D. Two Aspects of God's Will

Jesus reveals two ways in which a human being interacts with the Father's will. One consists in doing the will of God, the other consists in letting it be done.

(1) *Doing God's Will*

Jesus spoke of this first way with reference to his own mission:

> My food is to do [my Father's] will
> and to complete his work (John 4:34).

The perennial question, however, is this: What does God will specifically in a given situation? That question can prove extremely difficult to answer. The New Testament contains two statements which express apodictically what God wills:

> The will of [my Father]
> is that I should lose nothing of all that he has given me

and that I should raise it up on the last day (John 6:39).
The Lord wills no one to perish,
   but rather everyone to come to repentance (2 Pet 3:9).

Yet, even those texts are open to interpretation regarding just how universal "nothing," "no one" and "everyone" are in the concrete.

When we do God's will, *we* are the agents. We are the ones who intentionally and voluntarily set about accomplishing what we perceive that will to be. It is, therefore, in this context that we speak most accurately of discernment. When the Lord wishes us to do something, God must indicate somehow what that is. God alone can reveal to us what God desires. Discernment then is the faith process whereby we become conscious of the Father's will. Within a dialectic of searching and listening, probing and receiving, discernment unfolds according the the degree of enlightenment which God affords and to the extent that we are capable of assimilating God's will.

Because discernment begins in faith, proceeds in faith and ends in faith, it remains always shrouded in darkness. We cannot "know" with scientific precision what the Lord desires.

Thus, rather than say that such and such *is* the will of God, it seems more appropriate to affirm that a particular choice is *in the direction* of God's will. The divine will cannot be reduced to human categories. God's will infinitely transcends anything we can conceive it to be.

This question then arises: Is the belief that we are proceeding in the direction of God's will sufficient for lifelong commitment? Do we not need more assurance than that? Do we not have to be certain of what God desires before we make a permanent commitment? Since we can never possess empirical certitude in matters of faith, our discernment always retains an element of darkness and risk. Moreover, faith guides us through this night "more surely than the light of noonday."[5] Thus, the vocational imperative which moves us to lifelong commitment is produced by God in us, not precisely by

[5]St. John of the Cross, Poem: *In a Dark Night*, stanza 4. See *O Blessed Night*, 89–94, 147–150; *Receptivity*, 49–53, 97–101.

our conviction of proceeding in the direction of God's will. That conviction is rather the effect of the divine activity within us. In other words, instead of the signs guiding us, God moves us forward in our vocation; and, in the process, signs appear—signs which confirm and affirm.

(2) *Letting God's Will Be Done*

Jesus spoke of this second way of interacting with the Father's will in the context of his obedience unto death:

> Abba . . . remove this cup from me.
> Nevertheless, not what I will,
>   but what you will be done (Mark 14:36).

Moreover, Jesus specifically urged us to pray:

> Father . . . may your will be done
>   on earth as it is in heaven (Matt 6:10).

In letting God's will be done, we are no longer the agent; God is. It is the Lord who works through us and sometimes in spite of us.

In this context, we frequently fail not only to know what the Lord is effecting with us, but even to know whether God is accomplishing anything at all. Generally, we remain completely in the dark. It is often difficult enough to do God's will. But it is usually even more arduous to let the Lord's will be done. Our perceptions of it vary. Sometimes we have the impression of being dragged along frightened and bewildered, kicking and screaming. At other times we experience peaceful serenity in letting God's will be done.

Strictly speaking, discernment has little directly to do with letting the Lord's will be done. What the Father is bringing to pass remains solely his business (Luke 2:49). God chooses to ask of us only the general faith disposition of letting be accomplished whatever God desires, however the Lord wills it done. In this instance, God wills our cooperation by way of passivity rather than activity. In this context, rather than trying to produce anything ourselves, it is better for us not to know than to know; better to let go, let be, let the Lord act.

E. God's Willing and Our Will

The usual expression is "God's will." It is, however, theologically more accurate to say "God's willing." The progressive-verbal-noun comes closer to the truth than the simple noun, even if in English the latter sounds better.

Our will is clearly distinct from our willing. Our will is a capacity within us, an enduring capability, which we sometimes activate and at other times let lie dormant. God, on the other hand, wills eternally; God is always willing.

How does the Lord's willing affect our will? God moves us to move ourselves freely. God's willing moves our will to freely desire what God wills for us. Because we are free, a wide range of responses are possible. Sometimes we experience our freedom with spontaneity and joy. At other times we find our freedom perplexing and painful. Yet, the Lord works with each response, drawing us, transforming us. When we say "yes," the Lord incites us to deeper commitment. When we insist on "no," God works towards conversion. When we persist with "maybe," the Lord prods us out of indecision.

How can we be really free yet do what God desires? The fact is, we do not always do what the Lord wills. Moreover, even when we set out to accomplish the Father's will as we discern it, we rarely apply ourselves with the intensity and generosity desired by God.

Evangelical freedom is a more restricted concept than choice. We can choose good, evil or something between. Freedom, on the other hand, is expressed only in relation to good. We exercise our freedom to the extent that we act in view of the greatest good possible under the circumstances. Sin is therefore not a use of freedom, but an abuse of it.

How can we be truly free, if we cannot do what we want? What many people in Western society call "freedom" is in fact license. We want what we want when we want it. Moreover, we desire all this regardless of its effect on others. "This is my land, so I can do with it whatever I please!" "This is my car, therefore I can drive it any way I want!" "I'm paying for this electricity, so I can waste it however I like!" Those attitudes do not reflect freedom, but blatant self-centeredness.

The Lord moves us to choose freely what God has always destined for us. Clearly, the Lord wills the best for us. God desires to transform us in God, to divinize us. Moreover, with all our being we ourselves long for fullness of life in God. For this we were made, and our hearts remain forever restless until we rest in that which God wills that we freely will. True freedom, therefore, means choosing this destiny.

The Lord does not force or coerce us, yet God most surely pursues and, if need be, overpowers us (Jer 20:7-9). The Lord does not manipulate or trick us, but neither will God let us get away indefinitely with resistance (Gen 32:23-32). The Lord persists in working with our freedom until we are free enough to choose rightly. We grow into this maturity through gradually letting go our addictions, defense mechanisms, codependency and attachments (Ezek 36:24-28).

Frequently, when we want something, we demand it. If we do not get it immediately, we fight or connive until we do. This is not freedom. It is iron-fisted intransigence. It is bullheadedness. It is, in fact, a form of violence in which we force our will upon others despite their preferences, rights or feelings—and sometimes, even despite all common sense and our own better judgment.

God's will never does violence to anyone at any time in any way (Jer 18:1-6). If we could ever succeed in definitively thwarting the Lord's will, then we would have inflicted supreme violence upon ourselves. The Lord is determined to somehow bring God's salvific will to fulfillment in us:

> Indeed, as the rain and the snow come down from the heavens
> and do not return without watering the earth
> and making it yield . . .
> so the word which goes forth from my mouth
> does not return to me empty.
> It carries out my will
> and succeeds in what it was sent to do (Isa 55:10-11).

God refuses to let anything definitively separate us from Christ:

> For I am certain of this:
> Neither death nor life;
> no angel, no prince;

CHAPTER 2

God's Willing, God's Calling, God's Caring

The will of God, our vocation and divine providence are intricately interlaced. In fact, those three mysteries converge upon one, which is the Lord's "purpose"—God's *próthesis* (Eph 1:11) or *eudokía* (Eph 1:5,9). Looking at the same mystery from our point of view, we name it our "destiny" or "predestination" which is according to the divine purpose (Eph 1:11).[1] The moving hymn of praise for the history of salvation in Ephesians (1:4-11) brings together the themes of choosing and predestining, will and purpose. Here is a sampling:

> Before the foundation of the world,
>   the Father *chose* us to be holy in Christ . . . (v. 4)
>   *predestining* us in love
>   to become his children through Jesus . . . (vv. 4-5).
> In all wisdom . . .
>   he revealed to us the mystery of his *will* . . . (vv. 8-9).
>   recapitulating everything in Christ . . .
>   according to the *purpose* he has for all things (vv. 10-11).

---

[1]The noun "predestination" is not found in Scripture, only the verb *proorízo*: to limit or to ordain beforehand (see Rom 8:29–30; Eph 1:5, 10). *Próthesis* can also be rendered: a setting beforehand, a predetermination. *Eudokía* can mean: good will, pleasure or favor.

A. Calling and Caring:
Two Manifestations of the Divine Will

What we ordinarily name our "vocation" is in reality a particular way of perceiving God's purpose for us. It designates the divine will as it relates to who the Lord desires us to be, how we are to become that unique person and what we are sent forth to do for God and others. Thus, the Lord wills us to be transformed in God, wills us to become our transformed selves through a certain lifestyle and wills us to accomplish some mission.

What we usually name "divine providence" is also a particular way of understanding God's purpose for us. It accentuates the Lord's tender caring in every detail of our daily life.[2]

Many people are accustomed to imagining God's calling as something specific, predetermined and absolute. Hence, they tend to think of vocation in terms of straight lines and clear-cut categories. Some callings may indeed develop that way, but must all vocations necessarily do so? We believe not.

The Lord is free to call in a specific way or in a general way. God can give someone a particular direction, lifestyle or ministry, or call a person in an undetermined manner. At times, the Lord seems to will beforehand specifically what we choose. For example, a particular man is called from his mother's womb to marry a certain woman. In that case, God brings about their meeting, causes them to be in love and unites them in a conjugal covenant. At other times, the Lord seems to will only a general direction, desiring that we make a choice out of a number of possibilities. God then cooperates with our choice and moves us forward in a manner consonant with it. For instance, a woman may be called to marriage in general, but the calling to marry a specific man may not occur until after they meet.

(1) God's Will and All That Happens

Does God not will everything? At least after the fact, must we not say that such and such was the Lord's will? Isn't everything that happens somehow the will of God?

Confusion of the Lord's will (taken in a general sense) with divine providence (understood as a particular way of viewing

[2]See *Spiritual Journey*, 21–32.

the implementation of that will) frequently underlies those questions. Certainly, everything is capable of being worked into God's providence. Not even the most heinous sin—Jesus' cruci-fixion, deicide—is without redeemable features. However, we do not believe that God wills everything that happens.

To permit something to happen when one could stop it, is this not to will it in some way? To keep silent when one could speak up, is this not to assent implicitly? Yes, in a sense. None-theless, we prefer to envisage God's permission and silence in the light of divine providence rather than as a direct application of God's will. The Lord's will is always towards the greatest good for each of us. God's caring works to integrate all the sin, pain and death of our mortal existence into the process of our personal deification. Thus, it does not suffice merely to repeat the classical formula: "God wills good directly, wills physical evil indirectly, only permits moral evil." From an evolutionary and relational perspective, we would add that divine providence works everything toward God's purpose by drawing unimagina-ble good out of evil.

Does God really will the injustice, pain and misery that plague us on every side? Can we actually say that the Lord in-tends someone to be inflicted with AIDS or cancer? That God desires someone be born demented or physically disabled? Our belief is that the Lord does not will any of this. God wills only good—in fact, the very best for each of us all the time. In the Fa-ther's infinite caring, however, he cooperates with every detail of our lives, turning sin, selfishness, suffering—even death—to inconceivable good. Not everything is immediately good, but in God's providence everything is capable of becoming a catalyst for good. We contribute to this mystery of divine caring by our efforts to let God transform the situation from within.[3]

Is not all this a matter of semantics? Call it "will" or "provi-dence," does it not boil down to the same thing? Not exactly. There is a question of accent and of situating the mystery in its proper theological context.

Divine providence affects us every instant of our sojourn, each step along the way, in every facet of our lives. Yet, that

[3]See *O Blessed Night*, 137–153, 163–165; *Receptivity*, 89–103, 120–121.

truth does not automatically imply that God specifically, absolutely and uniformly wills everything that happens. To be sure, nothing that was, is or shall be is outside the Lord's caring. But this fact does not necessarily suggest that everything exists as God wills it to be, that it develops how the Lord wills it to become, or that it is doing what God wills it to accomplish. Even should the Lord desire a specific situation, that does not mean that God wills all aspects of it. The Lord does not thereby have to want all details in the same way or to the same degree. God may not will some elements at all.

Two examples from the gospel illustrate some of these points. Jesus clearly willed that the rich young man sell what he owned and follow him. The man, however, declined. The context implies that neither got what he wished, at least not at that time (Matt 19:16-22). On another occasion, Jesus willed that the apostles go off to a secluded place by themselves and rest with him for a while. Yet, when they arrived there, it was teeming with people waiting for them. So Jesus changed his plans and addressed their needs even to the point of feeding them (Mark 6:30-44).

(2) *God's Will and Tolerance of Evil*

Why does the Lord allow adverse things to happen, if God truly does not desire them? First of all, we have to admit that both parts of that sentence are true. The Lord does allow many situations to occur which are not willed. But, is that not a contradiction? No. Neither for God nor for us.

We bear with a multitude of situations both within ourselves and in others which we neither like nor want. Tolerance is an evangelical value which presupposes the existence of moral and physical evil (Matt 13:24-30). Tolerance allows evil to persist, but it does so from the perspective of the following threefold faith conviction:

- Evil ultimately destroys itself.[4]

[4]This truth is sometimes referred to as the principle of the Cross. The crucifixion of Jesus was the epitome of all moral and physical evil in the universe inasmuch as creation succeeded in murdering its Creator. Jesus did not, however, allow evil to destroy him. He rose from the dead totally transformed in God. Thus, he did not destroy evil, strictly speaking. He did not have to. He let it de-

- The Lord is so caring and provident as to draw forth good from evil situations (Rom 8:28-39).
- Our human condition makes it impossible for us to attain complete maturity all at once (Phil 3:9-15). We have to wait to be saved (Rom 8:22-25).

Therefore, it does not suffice to say merely that the Lord allows evil. God is not passive or unaffected by evil, but rather works to bring good out of it. The Father uses sin, suffering and death as occasions to transform us and to recapitulate all creation in Christ (Col 1:15-20).

Furthermore, our perspective of what might be best remains sorely myopic. Our view is like peering at the underneath portion of a tapestry. We see a maze of loose ends and dangling threads. God, on the other hand, beholds the tapestry right side up with its flowing patterns and blending shades.

Yet, the question persists: Why did the Lord not make a better world? As paradoxical as it may seem, God has made the best possible world—best according to the divine purpose and will. That purpose is the evolution of all creation toward recapitulation in Christ. It is not so much that God created us imperfect and defective. Rather God made us vibrantly moving towards consummate perfection, "where death, tears or sadness shall be no more" (Rev 21:4). The Lord made the world in such a way that Father, Son and Spirit remain personally involved in its creation and re-creation, personally interacting and cooperating with our individual destinies.

B. Divine Cooperation, Divine Interaction

We know that for those who love God
God works with [*syn-ergeî*] them in all things for good.
These have been called according to God's purpose
(Rom 8:28).

The Greek compound verb which St. Paul uses in the above text sheds much light on the mystery of God's will. Literally, the

stroy itself in trying to destroy him. The same mystery is reincarnated in each of our individual lives, and it will continue to be played out collectively until the parousia. See *O Blessed Night*, 150–151; *Receptivity*, 100–101.

infinitive means "to work with, to cooperate with, to labor together with." The noun derived from this verb designates a fellow-worker, an associate, a coadjutor (Rom 16:3, 9, 21).

In the context of the divine will moving us, the obvious meaning of this compound verb is that the Lord assists us. God is the ultimate motivating and moving principle of all that we are and do. *Syn-ergei*, however, denotes much more than help and causality. It suggests also mutual cooperation and interaction.

That we cooperate with the divine will goes without saying. We cooperate with God's salvific activity within us and around us. That we interact with divine providence also goes without saying. We interact with God's tender caring for us every instant of each day. Our cooperation, however, is not always whole-hearted nor is our interaction consistently positive. We sin more often than we like to admit.

Yet, can we say also that the Lord cooperates with us? That God interacts with us? We believe not only that we can but also that we must. Clearly, that assertion carries with it far-reaching implications, many of which may prove irreconcilable with a view of God's will as merely absolute, immutable and uniform.

The question can be restated thus: Do God's cooperation and interaction with us have any personal effect upon God? We believe that they do indeed. This coaction and interaction would seem to leave the Lord somehow open and exposed before us. God's loving care for us appears to give rise to a certain vulnerability in God. Four notions—receptivity, relativity, responsiveness and dynamic energy—reveal something of that divine vulnerability.

(1) *Receptivity*

Many people think of God not only as supreme being, but also as supreme activity—the absolute first cause and prime mover. Those conceptualizations of God remain insightful, but they do not exhaust our capacity for understanding the Lord's interaction with us.

To affirm that God needs us, receives something from us, waits for us to respond, sounds blasphemous to some people. Yet, is not Jesus the compassion of the Father? Does God not truly care what happens to us? Does the Lord not hurt when we hurt (Luke 19:41-44), rejoice when we rejoice (Matt 18:12-14)? Do we not somehow make a difference not only to God's world and to God's providence, but also to God? Yes, we must; otherwise how can the incarnation and redemption have a personal meaning?

To be receptive, to listen to another are not only created virtues but also uncreated qualities. We receive everything from the Lord (1Cor 4:7), and somehow in the divine purpose God receives from us. In some mysterious way we enhance the glory of God. Every positive act we make is capable of being *ad majórem Dei gloriam* (1 Cor 10:31).[5] God is receptive to our love and to us because God wills it so.

(2) *Relativity*

To the human mind, absolute and relative are antonyms. A thing cannot be both absolute and relative at the same time, under the same circumstances. Surely, the Lord is supremely absolute and utterly self-sufficient. However, God can be also transcendently relative.

We discover vestiges of this truth within the Trinity. The distinctions of the divine persons are predicated upon relatedness. The person of the Father is recognizable by a generative relationship with the Son. The person of the Holy Spirit is distinguishable by a spirated relatedness to the Father and the Son. In this way, we can speak of a transcendent relativity existing within the very absoluteness of the Godhead.

Certainly, the whole cosmos is related to God as Creator. Moreover, science is becoming increasingly aware of the interrelatedness of all elements of the universe. Yet, how can we say that God relates with creation—especially with human persons?

An initial response is this: Father, Son and Spirit are personally involved in creation. Not only does the Trinity relate to us, but also God's will relates to our existential situation. The divine will is an integral part of our daily life rather than apart from it. Whenever we exercise our will, an aspect of God's own will is set

---

[5]The Latin phrase, sometimes abbreviated AMDG, means "to the greater glory of God." It is the motto of the Jesuits and has been adopted by countless persons the world over.

in motion. We possess our capacity for willing because we have been given a participation in God's willing. Yet, the divine will remains somehow relative to our willing—relative to its stops and starts, to its hesitations and vacillations, to its positive impulses and negative influences.

In order to decide on a course of action, does God wait until we have first made up our mind? Is the Lord dependent on our whims? The images conjured up in those questions represent gross anthropomorphisms. However, if there is real interaction between the Lord and us, there must be also some form of transcendent relativity on the part of God's will toward ours. For:

- When we say "yes," the Lord does incite us further.
- When we say "no," God does work to convert us.
- When we say "maybe," the Lord does prod us forward.

The particular mode of God's cooperation with us is somehow related to our specific response to the divine initiative.

(3) *Responsiveness*

To respond means to do something in return to another: to answer, to react. Responsiveness occurs when someone's feelings, thoughts or actions elicit in us related feelings, thoughts or actions.

Scripture is replete with instances where God responds to the human situation. In the second account of creation, for example, Yahweh vigorously reacts to the sin of Adam and Eve (Gen 3:8-19). Abraham is presented as bargaining so well with the Lord that God backs down before the destruction of Sodom and Gomorrah (Gen 18:16-33). Intercessory prayer implies a certain responsiveness from the Lord (Matt 7:7-11). For those who believe in the possibility of damnation, their theology necessarily includes a post factum response by God to sinfulness (Matt 25:31-46). For surely, no one is predestined to reprobation (Rom 8:29).

We need to interpret the above biblical references, and others like them, in the light of pertinent exegetical and theological principles. Nonetheless, apart from the anthropomorphisms involved, those passages do indicate a responsiveness on God's part. This responsiveness does not detract from the Lord's transcendence. It does, however, make God much closer to us in terms of intimacy and caring.

Let us now speak really anthropomorphically. Responsiveness would appear to make life more difficult for God. "More difficult" in the sense that it seems much simpler for the Lord to predetermine and preprogram everyone and everything—the perfect software for the cosmic computer.

In a hierarchical mode of leadership, most rulers would agree that it is easier to dictate behavior to subordinates than to work, cooperate and interact with them. It is difficult for a leader to follow, to respond to a disciple's response. Yet, the kenotic principle of the incarnation teaches us just how responsive God is: "For Christ emptied himself assuming the condition of a servant" (Phil 2:7). Jesus does not treat us as a king would a subject, but rather as a servant does the one he has come to serve (John 13:2-14), as the beloved does his lover (John 15:9). God does not predetermine or preprogram us. Rather the Lord moves us to respond freely to the divine initiative. God remains lovingly, caringly, intimately responsive to our response.

Listening is one of the more expressive ways in which God's responsiveness manifests itself. The Lord listens to us—not only to what we say and want, but most especially to all that we are and are becoming in God. We do not, however, envisage divine responsiveness as a "wait and see" attitude, but rather as an involved, incarnated, committed dialogue of Beloved with lover. The Lord is never a laid-back disinterested observer. God does not give us a free will and a destiny to work out solely on our own. The Lord is there from beginning to end (Rev 22:13). God not only motivates and moves us, but also cooperates and interacts with us in every facet of our being and becoming. The Lord is a most interested participant in our individual and collective salvation/transformation.

(4) *Dynamic Energy*

Since there is so much change in us, is there a sense in which we can predicate change in God? At first sight, the Letter of James would indicate not:

> Every good and all perfection are from the Father

in whom there is no change or shifting shadow (Jas 1:17).

Surely, there is no vacillation or whim in God. A "change of heart" is out of the question. To say that the Lord might experience a "change of mind" sounds grossly anthropomorphic. Yet, the parabolic Book of Jonah includes the following thought in the Ninevites king's decree to his nobles:

> Who knows? God may yet relent [i.e., have a change of mind] and with compassion turn from fierce anger (Jonah 3:9).

We prefer not to use the word "change" at all in relation to God. We opt instead for "dynamism" and "energy" in the Pauline sense of *dýnamis* (Rom 15:19; 1 Cor 2:5; Eph 1:19). In God there is dynamic movement "from glory to glory" (2 Cor 3:18), meaning that somehow perfection renews itself in perfection.

Yet, if we do not turn out as the Lord wills—supposing that we have some idea of that will in the first place—does the Lord not have to change something in our regard? Yes, indeed. God changes us. The Lord converts us (Jer 18:1-6). That is, God moves us to freely allow ourselves to be changed (Mark 1:15; 2 Cor 3:18). Truly, the Lord "predestines" us (Rom 8:28). However, God does so not in a static preprogrammed way, but in an open evolving manner which responds to our responses. In the day-to-day interactions between the divine will and ours, it is possible that the Lord wills to adapt to our developing situation. God's will responds and reacts to, cooperates and interacts with our changing will in a thousand-and-one different ways, as each situation warrants.

CHAPTER 3

The Will of God and Vocation

God's will is not only transcendent but also immanent. Viewed from an evolutionary and relational perspective, that immanence includes on the part of the divine will a certain vulnerability to our use or misuse of freedom. Thus, the Lord's will is receptive and responsive to us as we say "yes," "no" or "maybe" to God's initiative.

Vocation is an aspect of the Lord's will as it applies to our developing life situation. God does not impose anything on us—not even divinization. Rather, the Lord interacts and cooperates with us every step of the way, eliciting our free response to the destiny to which God has gratuitously called us.

Neither "God's will" nor "vocation" is a univocal concept. That is, neither has exactly the same meaning on every occasion. Both notions can have diverse suppositions under different circumstances. Father, Son and Spirit interact with each of us in a uniquely personal manner at every moment of our existence. There is no single uniform way in which the Lord motivates and moves everyone. Thus, no matter how comprehensive a theology of the Lord's will and vocation may be, God's freedom of election and our freedom of choice inevitably introduce some wrinkle, some exception. We, therefore, have to beware of oversimplifications and sweeping generalizations. Yet, we do perceive certain basic patterns within this singularity and diversity. These commonalities are the focus of our considerations. Spiritual directors, on a one-to-one basis with their directees, need to adapt these principles to each particular discernment.

A. A Complex Example

How then might we describe the interaction of God's will and our vocation throughout the gradual unfolding of our destiny?

One of the most complex examples imaginable is the vocational lifestyle of marriage. The supposition is this: the Lord wills that two individuals live together in a bond so intimate that the personal transformation of each is worked out in direct relationship with the other.

(1) *Basic Principles Regarding Vocation and God's Will*

Before we tackle the example of a vocation to marriage, we wish to enunciate several basic principles. These statements form the backdrop against which we explore the situation at hand. Since we treat all these principles at length in this book, we state them here as briefly as possible. They are:

(a) The Lord gifts each of us with a fundamental direction and destiny from the instant that we are brought into being.[1] God does this in conjunction with the co-creative activity of our parents. The basic lineaments of our vocation and our initial act of existence are in many respects coextensive. Yet, the Lord does not necessarily bestow all dimensions of vocation at the same time as existence. The Lord gives them and coordinates their development in God's own way and in God's own time for each individual.

(b) While at times the divine will may indeed focus on something precise, more often God's will seems to operate as a dynamic web of interrelating and integrating actions and responses. God's focus is holistic. The Lord's will attains the whole, the parts and the relationships among them. Yet, God does not necessarily will all aspects uniformly. The actualization of the Lord's will remains inextricably complex and mysterious.

(c) While on occasion the divine will may indeed be specific, much of the time it appears general. It seems to be relative and responsive to the interaction of God's freedom and our choices.

(d) Each calling is a unique personal grace as well as an invitation to serve others. Therefore, a vocation transcends the clas-

[1] See *Spiritual Journey*, 40–45.

sifications and the institutionalizations which our minds and society use to identify and to actualize it. As helpful as those categories and institutions remain, God's calling, nonetheless, exceeds their limitations. The richness and complexity of a vocation cannot be simply reduced to, entirely expressed in or fully exhausted by definitions or delineations, no matter how appropriate. For example: When God calls two people to marry, that vocation surpasses what the specific articles on matrimony in *The Code of Canon Law* are capable of capsulizing.

(e) Whenever we deal with examples, we present them as succinctly as possible. Actual cases, however, involve innumerable variations and include countless factors. Reality is always more complex than we can imagine.

(2) *Possible Scenarios*

Let us now take up the example of marriage. An authentic calling to marry implies this: God wills that a man and a woman love one another and commit themselves to each other in a union so intimate as to shape the remainder of their salvation history. They voluntarily and completely surrender their singlehood in the interest of that deeper and wider life which they henceforth share in common.

For convenience's sake, we name our couple John and Jane. Our example unfolds in three scenarios. A virtually unlimited number of other possibilities are, however, conceivable. For the sake of brevity in these scenarios, we speak very anthropomorphically of God's action.

A first scenario. When the Lord initially brings John and Jane into being, God also gives them a vocation. The Lord calls each to a unique identity in God; calls them to marry one another; calls each to accomplish some mission. Yet, God does this not in a static preprogrammed way, but in a manner which interrelates and interacts with all the evolving facets of their individual lives.

One of the first tasks for the Lord is to cause John and Jane to meet so that they can become conscious of their calling to marry each other. That task is simplified if they both attend the same school. But what if one grows up in New York and the other in California?

On the one hand, God may subtly prompt Jane to make certain options which will lead her eventually to meet John. Their respective chemistries then begin to work, they come to love each other, and they move toward marriage. On the other hand, God may modify or adapt certain external circumstances, thereby causing them to meet. In other words, there is no telling how divine providence brings about a "chance" encounter. Yet, if the Lord wills that these two marry, they must somehow meet and grow in love.

A second scenario. In the first example, we supposed that from the initial act of existence God willed John and Jane to marry each other. But is it not also possible that God could give John and Jane from their inception[2] a vocation to marriage in general, without calling the one to marry the other until after they had met? Certainly. The general vocation to marry does not have to coincide from the outset with a calling to marry a specific person.

In this second scenario, John and Jane will gradually awaken to their vocations to marriage. Pursuing that general calling, they will probably date many people. In time they meet, mature in love and decide to marry each other. In this supposition, God does not bring them together in accord with a prenatal plan, but rather lets nature take its course, so to speak. The Lord gives them a specific vocation to one another only after they have met. Had they never met, God might well have given each a calling to marry someone else.

A third scenario. There is still another way—and who knows how many more—to imagine the situation. At inception, God may gift John and Jane with a general direction toward deification without simultaneously also bestowing the seed of or even the direction toward a specific lifestyle or mission. For God's own purpose, the Lord may grant these gifts only later in life.

[2]Ordinarily, we use the term "inception" rather than "conception" to refer to the instant when God creates the human person within the matter prepared by the cocreative activity of one's parents. Many believe that this moment coincides with conception. Nonetheless, we wish to respect legitimately differing viewpoints. "Inception," therefore, means whenever the human person as such actually begins. See *Spiritual Journey,* 19.

Thus, in the first scenario Jane and John were destined from inception to marry each other. This case may be likened to an acorn which in time develops into a mighty oak. Everything the tree needs to become itself is contained in the seed from the outset.

In the second scenario, each person was called to marriage in general, with the specific vocation to wed one another coming only after they had met. This vocation to marry is similar to an uncharted trip in which particulars take shape in due course.

In the third scenario, neither one receives at inception more than a general direction toward God. The Lord specifies their vocational lifestyle and mission as their lives develop. This scenario is like the call of the wild in which they are impelled forward, while God interacts with every step and change of direction.

Each of the three scenarios would be immeasurably compounded if—before he experiences what he considers an authentic calling to marry Jane—John is ordained a Roman Catholic priest and assumes the canonical obligations of clerical celibacy. How are we to interpret the issue of vocational lifestyle when God seems to be calling—either from the womb or sometime later—a professed celibate to marriage?

Suppose, moreover, that Jane is already wedded at least nominally to someone else before she meets John. How do we interpret the situation in which a person is legally married to somebody other than the one with whom God appears to be calling her to spend the rest of her life?

We believe that God gives everyone some vocation at inception, at least a call to self-identity. Moreover, the Lord bestows in many persons from the instant of their individual creation the thrust of a basic lifestyle and a fundamental mission. Yet, God remains sovereignly free to work out all dimensions of our vocation in ways that we could never imagine:

> My thoughts are not your thoughts.
> My ways are not yours ways—
> this is Yahweh who speaks (Isa 55:8).

B. Concluding Thoughts Regarding the Will of God

In spite of the fact that every example clouds the truth to some degree, we hope that the above illustrations of God's will and vocation are more stimulating than confusing. There are clearly many more questions than answers. Important conclusions do, however, flow from the reflections which we have offered:

(1) The more detailed an example or situation is, the less our mind is capable of grasping specifically God's will or activity in it. Conversely, the more general our considerations remain, the better we can attain a sense of the direction of God's will. Our faith does seek that understanding no matter how limited it is.

(2) Usually, the more specific a situation is, the less we can be sure of God's will in it. All we can do in most instances is admit that a certain option now seems to be in the direction of the Lord's will for us. This fact does not, however, rule out the gradual formation of a spiritual imperative which can lead to lifelong commitment in a vocational lifestyle—marriage or celibacy, for example.

(3) Most of the time, we know better what God's will is not than what it is. We recognize more readily the directions which are not for us than we know precisely how to choose or what to do in concrete situations.

(4) On a minute-to-minute, hour-to-hour basis our intuition and common sense are two of the most significant means through which we perceive something of God's will. By intuition, we mean that innate capacity beyond reasoning and logic whereby we attain a grasp of the essential. Common sense, on the other hand, relates the insight attained by intuition to the rest of our existence. It relates the meaningfulness of a course of action to the other facets of our life. In the context of faith-imbued discernment, whenever intuition and common sense affirm a specific option, we can be confident that we are proceeding in the direction of God's will.

(5) In sincerely trying to pursue the will of God, we cannot make an irreparable mistake (Rom 8:28-39). We shall no doubt commit errors—perhaps even grievous ones (Rom 7:14-25)—

but the Lord will use everything to bring about unimaginable good (Rom 8:18, 28; 1 Cor 2:9).

(6) The more static and absolute, the more immutable and uniform we conceive God's will to be, the "easier" it is to fool ourselves into believing that we "know" that will. On the other hand, the more dynamic and relational, the more responsive and receptive we understand God's will to be, the more impossible it is to pin down precisely that will. An evolutionary approach to the will of God, vocation and lifelong commitment requires a more lively faith in Father, Son and Spirit.

GOD'S CALLING

CHAPTER 4

Chosen by God

God is utterly mysterious, a host of paradoxes. That truth is especially evident when our faith seeks to understand from an evolutionary and relational perspective something of God's dealings with us. From that perspective, the Lord is not only transcendent but also immanent, not only self-sufficient but also receptive, not only absolute but also relative, not only immutable but also responsive. God foreknows us in such a way as to cooperate with us in every detail of our lives, yet without forcing us. The Lord predestines us in such a manner as to interact with us every step of our journey, yet without preprogramming us. God has plans for us and sees that they are ultimately accomplished, yet without predetermining our response. God is infinite and eternal. We are immersed in space and time. Yet, the Lord remains enigmatically vulnerable to us here and now.

Those mysterious paradoxes apply in a special way to God's willing, caring and calling.

"Willing" refers to the Lord's purpose and our destiny. Sometimes we do the will of God. At other times we let it be done. Not only do we cooperate with the Lord and together with God actualize the divine purpose, but also the Lord interrelates with us in an inscrutably flexible manner.

"Caring," or providence, denotes an aspect of God's implementation of the divine will. The Lord does not will uniformly or necessarily in detail all that happens. Providence does, nonetheless, work everything to good for those who love God (Rom 8:28).

"Calling" addresses that dimension of divine willing which pertains to our vocation in this life. God wills that we attain the fullness of our *self-identity* by being divinized. As we journey toward the resurrection, that development ordinarily takes place within a certain *lifestyle* and encompasses a *mission*. Thus, when we use the word "vocation," we distinguish three components: *who* God calls us to be, *how* the Lord calls us to become our unique selves, *what* God calls us to do.

Several biblical themes converge on the mystery of vocation:

- election, or being chosen by God;
- calling, especially in the sense of called by name;
- consecration by God and unto God.

We treat these themes in four successive chapters. First then, what does it mean to be chosen by God?

A. Divine Election in the Hebrew Scriptures

The biblical notion of divine election is multifaceted.[1] For our purposes, we concentrate only on that data which bears on the mystery of vocation.

One key passage expressing Israel's consciousness of divine election is this:

> You are a people holy to the Lord your God. . . .
> The Lord has chosen you from among all the nations of the earth . . . solely out of love for you (Deut 7:6-8).

The Hebrew word for "to choose" is *bahár*. It means also to elect or to select. In an extended sense, it can imply sifting or separating as well as proving, examining or testing. In a passive construction, to be selected denotes choice of what is best or excellent. Generally speaking, *bahár* refers to a deliberate selecting which is occasioned by some need. Thus, the value of one's choice can be examined in the light of certain criteria.

(1) *Characteristics of Divine Election*

In some ninety-two instances in the Hebrew Scriptures, God is the subject of *bahár*. The Lord makes specific choices out of in-

[1]See *TDNT*, IV:144–192; *TDOT*, II:73–87.

numerable possibilities. For example, from among all the na-
tions of the earth the Lord selects Israel to be the people of God
(Deut 7:6). The act of choosing is utterly gratuitous on Yahweh's
part.

In some contexts, Hebrew prophetic literature uses *yadá* (to
know) where we would expect the verb "to choose." For instance, Yahweh reveals to Jeremiah: "Before I formed you in the
womb, I knew you" (Jer 1:5). Or, to Israel: "You alone have I
known from among all the peoples of the earth" (Amos 3:2).

In English, we do not ordinarily interchange knowing with
willing. Yet, the ancient Hebrew mentality on occasion employed *yadá* to emphasize a free and efficacious act of God's will
with regard to a certain person or group. *Yadá* then implies election. In these cases, however, we do sense a slight difference between knowing and choosing. *Yadá* accentuates the establishment of a covenant. *Bahár*, on the other hand, describes the
results of that initiative. Thus, knowing us so intimately and experiencing us so lovingly, Yahweh chooses us freely.

God's election is absolutely gratuitous. That gratuity stands
in stark contrast to the human exercise of selection. When we
choose, the rational element ordinarily dominates. We choose as
a consequence of reasoning on the subject. We select something
because it strikes us as favorable, good or worthy. Divine election, the other hand, transcends and sometimes defies all logic.
The Lord selects uniquely out of love:

> Yahweh chose you and set affection on you
>   not because you were more numerous than other
>   peoples . . .
>   but solely because Yahweh loved you (Deut 7:7-8).

God's election creates in us favorableness, goodness and
worth. It does not follow upon them. Prior to the Lord's choice,
there is literally nothing. It is Yahweh's love and fidelity—God's
heséd we-emét (Pss 25:10; 86:15)—rather than our lovableness
or envisaged faithfulness which motivate divine choice.

Since the Lord has chosen us out of love, it behooves us to
lovingly choose God in return. This response lies at the core of
the Hebrew notion of commitment. Having been elected, we are
accountable before the Lord for that incomparable gift. Out of

profound gratitude for having been chosen, we irresistibly yearn to respond to the divine initiative. The Book of Joshua, for example, uses *bahár* to describe our election of God in response to God's election of us:

> [Aware that the Lord has chosen you,] you experience within
>   yourselves your choice to serve Yahweh [in return] . . .
> Abandon your idols, therefore,
>   and surrender your heart to the Lord (Josh 24:22-24).

Among the prophets, only Deutero-Isaiah relates both election and calling to the granting of a mission. Election in this context is that out of which calling proceeds. Thus, Yahweh says of God's chosen one:

> [You are] my servant . . . my elect . . .
> I have called you to serve the cause of right . . .
>   to be a light to the nations (Isa 42:1, 6).

With the exception of Deutero-Isaiah, the prophets generally describe their calling rather than their election. If a distinction exists between these two actions which we attribute to God, it consists possibly in this: Election implies setting the chosen one apart. It accentuates a state of being. One is chosen to be holy. Divine calling, on the other hand, stresses mission. It connotes sending forth. One is called to accomplish something.

(2) *Divine Election: A Humbling Experience*

Conscious that the Lord had chosen them, certain Israelites developed an elitist attitude toward the rest of humanity: "Is not Yahweh among us? No evil can befall us" (Mic 3:11); "God is with us . . . we are secure" (Jer 5:12; 7:4, 10). They rejected other peoples, assuming that the Lord did not also guide their lives.

In reality, however, Yahweh's choice of Israel underscores the universality of salvation history (Amos 9:7). Although *bahár* implies separating, the Lord does so only to accentuate the relationship of service of the part to the whole, of the few to the many, of the one to the all.

Divine election does not establish dominion or primacy. It rather postulates responsibility toward others and faithful obedience to Yahweh. Because God so loved the whole world, God chose Israel for a special mission in universal salvation history.

Divine election is, therefore, a matter of faith experience, not logic. It is pure gift, not reward. It is cause for humility, not pride. Divine election does not establish dominion, but rather soul-searching accountability. It is an act of God's superabundant love for both one and all.

B. The Christian Sense of Election

The principal word which New Testament authors use to render *bahár* is *eklégomai*. They employ this verb only in the middle voice, which means that the agent (subject of the sentence) acts with reference to him/herself. Hence, Jesus is said to select for himself someone or something from among many possibilities. The accent "for himself" is not egotistical, however. The election is in view of a special grace, a personal favor or a mission to others. The fact that election is made out of a number of possibilities is present but not necessarily stressed.

Also significant in the New Testament are the adjective *eklektós* (chosen, selected, exalted, precious) and the noun *eklogé* (election, the elect, the aggregate of those who are chosen).

(1) *The Synoptics*

In two key passages, Luke presents Jesus as God's Elect. At the transfiguration the Father proclaims: "This is my Son, my chosen one" (Luke 9:35). The scoffing Jews at the foot of the cross entice Jesus: "He saved others. Let him save himself if he is the Christ of God, the chosen one" (Luke 23:35). After his resurrection, Jesus reveals to his disciples that his passion and death marked the chosen point of transition into his glory (Luke 24:26, 46). Thus, Luke treats Jesus's divine election in conjunction with his paschal mystery and salvific mission.

The Gospel according to Matthew contains one of Scripture's most paradoxical statements regarding divine election: "Many are called, but few are chosen" (Matt 22:14). This logion concludes the parable of the wedding feast in Matthew (22:2-14), but is omitted by Luke in a parallel passage (Luke

14:16-24). Mark does not mention either the logion or the parable.

Matthew 22:14 highlights the necessity for unconditional submission to the Lord by the recipients of God's election. Even the person without a wedding garment is chosen. But because s/he brings disobedience to the celebration and does not exhibit conduct which corresponds to Yahweh's blessing, s/he cannot be a full participant. Obedience and faith create the interior disposition in which God brings election to fulfillment.

Divine election takes place within the interplay of real life. It is not static or theoretical. It elicits accountability and commitment. Thus, the sense of Jesus's logion is: Of all those who were invited, only a few—a remnant—have lived up to the full demands of their election.

(2) The Fourth Gospel

In the Gospel according to John, election is related especially to the problem of Judas. How could he be a chosen apostle and yet betray Jesus? John addresses the situation in three stages: (a) Jesus poses the problem: "Have I not chosen you, the Twelve? Yet, one of you is a demon" (John 6:70). (b) At the Last Supper, the Master explains: "I know whom I have chosen. But this is to fulfill the scripture. . . . " (John 13:18). (c) Finally, the Lord gives the full development of his thought on election after Judas leaves: "You did not choose me. No, I chose you, and I commissioned you to go forth and to bear lasting fruit" (John 15:16). "I have chosen you out of the world" (John 15:19).

Characteristic of the above statements is the fact that Jesus himself does the electing. Moreover, he chooses deliberately. His election of Judas was not a mistake. He chose Judas to be an apostle, not a traitor. His election was positive, not negative.

In biblical narratives we find Hebraisms which translators sometimes render "so that. . . . " In the original idiom, these expressions indicate frequently not so much ordained purpose as emphatic statement of fact. They assert: "That's the way it turned out!" It is in this sense that Jesus alludes to the fulfillment of Psalm 41:9 in relation to Judas (John 13:18): "Even my closest and most trusted friend—one who shared my table—rebelled against me." Although Jesus knew beforehand that Judas would be the traitor (John 6:70), he was not foreordained to be so.

Personal accountability and commitment are the core of our response to God's election. The Lord works out that election in the context of our faith and infidelity, our listening and disobedience. God's will concretized in divine election remains receptive, relative and responsive to our response.

(3) *The Pauline Corpus*

Speaking of the community which God has chosen in Corinth, the Apostle to the Gentiles describes how the Lord has taken what is foolish and weak to confound the world's wisdom and power (1 Cor 1:27-29).

The Letter to the Ephesians emphasizes both the Father's gratuity and purpose in election: "He chose us in Christ Jesus before the creation of the world to be holy" (Eph 1:4).

The noun "election" is not used frequently in the Pauline corpus. On two occasions, however, there is reference to the members of the Christian community as "the chosen of God" (Rom 8:33 and Col 3:12). In those texts the aim of election is *agápe*—the love of the Lord for us, our love for God and our love for one another. The author of Colossians addresses the elect—that is, the entire Christian fellowship—as those who are "holy and beloved of God."

(4) *Election according to the First Letter of Peter*

While virtually every New Testament author speaks of divine election, the First Letter of Peter makes it a principal theme. The epistle begins:

> To God's elect, to you pilgrims . . . who are chosen
>   according to the foreknowledge of the Father,
>   to be made holy by the Spirit,
>   in obedience . . . to Jesus Christ:
> Grace and peace be yours in abundance (1 Pet 1:1-2).

The addressee is the whole Christian community, especially those Gentiles living in certain provinces of Asia Minor. Those elect are figuratively aliens dispersed over the face of the earth.

Nonetheless, they are also "a chosen people, a royal priesthood, a holy nation, a multitude belonging to God" (1 Pet 2:9).

According to this letter, election begins with the foreknowledge of the Father—a foreknowledge which exists "from the foundation of the world" (1 Pet 1:20). Election then is not only pre-merit but also pre-temporal. Although it unfolds in space and time, it exists from all eternity and will last for all eternity. Divine foreknowledge, however, does not cause a static, robotized, preprogrammed response on the part of the elect. It rather draws human freedom and human spontaneity toward their maximum fulfilment. The Lord moves us to move ourselves freely and inexorably toward God.[2]

God's election of us is a Trinitarian action. It originates with the Father who chooses the Son to become incarnate (1 Pet 1:20). In Jesus, the Father chooses us also. That choice constitutes us the elect in his Elect—his sons and daughters in his Son. Furthermore, the Father chooses us "to be made holy in the Spirit" (1 Pet 1:2), who is, as it were, the agent bringing election to fruition.

As recipients of divine election, we actualize this gift by "obedience to Jesus Christ" (1 Pet 1:2). Etymologically, "to obey" in both Hebrew and Greek comes from the verb "to listen."[3] Faithful listening to God, or the lack of it, is ultimately our response to his choice of us.

We are living stones in Christ, chosen by God to build a spiritual home (1 Pet 2:5). Divine election rejects no one. However, sometimes we try to spurn our election (1 Pet 2:4; John 1:11). Thus, the stone which the builders rejected—but which in reality became the keystone as God's Elect—becomes a stumbling block for the disobedient (1 Pet 2:6-8).

C. Summary: The Universality of Divine Election

As God began to reveal the mystery of divine election—grounded in eternity but operative in living history—certain currents of Hebrew thought tended to conceive of this choice in terms of nationalistic pride and sectarian restriction. Many

[2]See *Spiritual Journey,* 21–30.
[3]See *Spiritual Direction,* 176.

prophets tried to correct that view, for they were convinced of the universality of Yahweh's love. Moreover, they readily recognized that Israel was chosen for a special responsibility in mediating the consciousness of that love to all people.

Nowhere does Scripture teach that God ever rejected anyone or any group of persons. The Lord chooses no one for reprobation. On the contrary, God destines all to transforming union in Christ Jesus. The Father calls everyone to be made holy by the Spirit. In a real sense, therefore, God chooses, selects and elects each human being by virtue of his/her individual creation. The Father chooses each of us to exist. He selects us out of unimaginable possibilities. However, he does not merely bring us into existence. Having chosen each one to be, God also selects everyone to become divinized. The Father elects us in his Elect. We respond to this mystery by decisive listening to God and by committed faith in Christ Jesus.

The revelation of the universality of divine election becomes the foundation for what is termed "the universal call to holiness."[4] Both of these mysteries then constitute the basis for belief in the universality of salvation. For

> God, [the Father], so loved the world
> that he gave his only Son . . .
> so that through him the world might be saved
> (John 3:16-17).

Or, as Jesus himself expresses it:

> The will of the one who sent me [i.e., the Father]
> is that I should lose nothing
> of all that he has given to me,
> and that I should raise it up on the last day (John 6:39).

The ecclesial dimension of those mysteries postulates that the Father has chosen the Christian community in his Son and with his Spirit to mediate until the parousia a certain aspect of his everlasting love for the whole human race. God has selected a particular group for the benefit of the elect at large. God does not display preferential treatment for a few over all others.

---

[4]See "The Dogmatic Constitution on the Church," *The Documents of Vatican II*, 39–42; *Contemplation*, 13–20.

CHAPTER 5

Called by God

God is one. God is simple. "God is Spirit" (John 4:24). Yet, in order to arrive at some understanding of the Lord's mysterious dealings with us, we ascribe successive acts to God. Respecting our human modes of cognition, the Lord has throughout history revealed to humankind several interrelated notions which help us appreciate something of how vocation comes about.

First, God knows us. The New Testament names this "foreknowledge"—*prógnosis* (1 Pet 1:2). The Lord knows us even before we exist (Jer 1:5). Knowing us from all eternity, God brings us into being in space and time. That divine activity makes us knowable and lovable to ourselves and others.

Then, knowing us, God chooses us. Divine election means deliberate choice in love. This election accentuates a state of being: "You are holy to Yahweh . . . The Lord your God has chosen you" (Deut 7:6). It indicates also an intention on God's part to cause us to become more.

Now, having foreknown and chosen us, God calls us. Call thus complements election. Divine calling in Scripture is frequently related to unexpected mission. An individual may be called to do something out of the ordinary, to accomplish a task previously unimagined. For instance, God called the child Samuel who did not yet know Yahweh to warn Eli the prophet of impending disaster (1 Sam 3:1-18). The Lord called a reluctant Jeremiah to preach the imminent destruction of Judah and Jerusalem (Jer 1-25). Jesus called the rich young man to give up his opulent lifestyle and follow him (Matt 19:16-22).

A. Called by Name: Isaiah 43:1

The mystery of divine calling pervades the Hebrew Scriptures. One passage in particular expresses the gist of all Old Testament revelation on the subject:

> Thus says Yahweh,
>   who created you, Jacob,
>   and who formed you, Israel . . .
> I have called [*qarathí*] you
>   by your very own name [*be-shim-ká*];
>   you are mine [*li-atáh*] (Isa 43:1).

(1) *"To Call" in Hebrew*

The verb in question is *qará*, whose most primitive meaning is to cry out or to shout aloud. It signifies also invoking, proclaiming, celebrating, inviting, summoning, convoking. In a more personal sense, it means to call or to name—to call by name. When placed on the mouth of Yahweh, *qará* reveals something of the mystery which we have come to identify as "vocation."

To the Western mind, the phrase *qará be-shém*—to name by name—seems tautologous. For the Hebrew, however, that redundancy is not needless repetition but theological insistence. It is an assertion of God's initiative in establishing a covenant with an individual. Moreover, the expression in Isaiah 43:1 reads *be-shim-ká*, which is "by your very own name." The phrase thus implies the utmost intimacy possible.

The Lord's invitation to participate in the inner life of God is absolutely gratuitous. Yahweh bestows this gift not because of our goodness or worthiness—whether actual or foreseen—but solely out of unconditional love. That abiding love draws us irresistibly to give way to the divinizing activity within us. Thus, the calling is to God as God, rather than to some place or state: heaven or happiness, for example.

The sentence "you are mine" emphasizes the interpersonal nature of calling. Literally, the Hebrew reads: "to me, you." The preposition *le* ("to") denotes at the same time motion toward, belonging to and longing for another. By calling us, Yahweh implants in our inmost being an innate thrust toward God. That mysterious drive—within us, but not of us—constitutes the quintessence of our spiritual direction.[1] We continue to experience that restless yearning with an ever increasing intensity until we find ourselves totally surrendered to the Lord.

(2) *To Be Called by One's Very Own Name*

In Isaiah 43:1, it is significant that Yahweh does not call us generically but specifically. The Lord calls us by name; indeed, by our very own name. To be thus called is to be known eternally and to be chosen to exist in time. It is to be created as a unique individual. It is to be loved intimately, personally and faithfully by God. To be called by our own name is to be espoused to the Lord. It is to be drawn into a covenant with God. It is ultimately to be invited to become one with God in participant transformation, while at the same time attaining the pinnacle of self-identity.

God's call creates each of us into a unique person with a particular way to reach full maturity in Christ. We receive a singular identity as well as the potential to attain maximum development of our personhood. We receive the power to experience, to know and to love the Lord. Integral to the Lord's calling us by name then is the mystery of our being and becoming in God. The Lord has implanted within us a thrust toward the fullness of being: eternal life in God. Our being has a dynamic propensity toward ever greater becoming. To be is to become God by participation. To be fully human is to become divinized.[2]

(3) *Having One's Name Changed*

Isaiah 43:1 brings out the creative and the re-creative aspects of divine calling in the expression:

> Yahweh, who created you, Jacob,
> and who formed you, Israel (Isa 43:1).

Literally, the Hebrew reads: "Yahweh creating you, Jacob; forming you, Israel." The use of the active participle in both verbs emphasizes that the divine activity is ongoing. The change from the verb "creating" in the first instance to "forming" in the second is significant. The verse is an example of synthetic parallelism,

[1]See *Spiritual Direction*, 15–32.
[2]See *Contemplation*, 16–18.

typical of Hebrew poetry. That is, the second stich repeats the thought of the first, yet adds a further insight.

Thus, the first stich, "creating you, Jacob," refers to God's initial call into being. The second stich, "forming you, Israel," while repeating the preceding thought, alludes to the dynamic, evolutionary dimension in creation—the fact that being means becoming more than what presently is.

The second stich indicates something of the re-creative force of divine love. This indication occurs in the change of name from Jacob which means "following after" (Gen 25:26) to Israel which means "ruling with God" (Gen 32:28; 35:10). In Semitic thought, Yahweh changes a name to indicate the effecting of an interior transformation.

(4) *Divine Resolve*

A final aspect of divine call as exemplified in Isaiah 43:1 pertains to divine resolve. Even though the process of being transformed reaches completion only in the future, the Hebrew text describes this process as already accomplished: "I have called" you (*qarathí*). The verb is in the perfect qal stem, thus describing a simple completed action.

Couched in the Semitic verb form is this truth: God so intends to bring the calling to completion that God sees the work as already accomplished. Yahweh persistently and irresistibly seeks out the person called, until finally that individual surrenders freely and totally to God in love.

B. The Christian Sense of Calling

Like the Hebrew *qará*, the New Testament *kaléo*[3] is a special term designating an activity of God within the process of sanctification.

God is always the one who exercises, whether directly or indirectly, the initiative in calling us. For instance, Romans 9:12 speaks of the Lord's freedom of choice "since it depends on the one who calls, rather than on human merit." Romans 4:17 describes God as one "calling into being that which does not yet

[3]See *TDNT*, III:487–501.

exist." Moreover, Paul assures us: "The one calling you is always faithful" (1 Thess 5:24).

As in the Hebrew Scriptures, the Lord calls a person to God above all (1 Thess 2:12; 2 Thess 2:13-14). Yet, the Lord also calls people to accomplish certain tasks, to fulfill specific missions. Jesus calls his disciples to bear lasting fruit (John 15:16) and to endure the sufferings of the apostolate to which they are sent (1 Pet 2:20-21).

The New Testament revelation of the Trinity adds further insight to the notion of vocation.

"God [the Father] has called [us] into communion with his Son" (1 Cor 1:9). Thus, we belong to Christ (Rom 1:6) and participate in the divine sonship of Jesus: "The Father lets us be called children of God, for indeed we are" (1 John 3:1). Yet, the Father's calling of us in Christ remains in accordance with "God's purpose in election" (Rom 9:11).

Christ himself is called by name through the power of the Spirit. Mary is told: "You shall bear a son and you shall call his name Jesus" (Luke 1:31). Similarly, God revealed to Joseph: "Mary will bear a son and you will call his name Jesus" (Matt 1:21).

Christ calls all his disciples to him: "Come, follow me" (Matt 16:24; 19:21). That is, he calls them not only to follow his example and to live his teaching, but also to come to *himself*, to encounter him personally.

The gospel contains accounts of the manner in which Jesus called certain individuals: his first followers (John 1:35-50), Levi (Luke 5:27-28), Paul (Acts 9:1-19), etc.

Christ calls disciples in his own name as well as in the Father's name: "He called to himself the Twelve" (Matt 10:1); "I did not come to call the virtuous but sinners" (Matt 9:13). There are persons whom Jesus calls specifically by name: each of the apostles (Luke 6:13-16), Cephas (John 1:42), Martha (Luke 10:41), Zacchaeus (Luke 19:5), Lazarus (John 11:43), Mary Magdalen (John 20:16), etc.

To be called by God is ultimately to be invited to receive the Trinity within us and thereby to enter into the process of transforming union. To be called is to be drawn to surrender what is deepest, most ineffable and loving in us to that which is deepest, most ineffable and loving in Father, Son and Spirit. To be called is to be destined to consummate loving communion wherein we are "filled with the utter fullness of God" (Eph 3:19).

C. New Testament Derivatives

Three significant derivatives of *kaléo* are found in the New Testament, especially in Paul. These words afford further insight into God's calling and our vocation.

(1) *Klésis: Calling*

This verbal noun is usually translated "calling," rather than "call." It is the New Testament equivalent of "vocation." *Klésis*, furthermore, refers to the state of having been called by God which results from unmerited election (2 Tim 1:9). In this sense, it approximates "chosen."

Paul uses *klésis* to emphasize the Lord's fidelity in bringing the divine call to completion: "The gifts and the calling of God are irrevocable" (Rom 11:29). The same word is employed to exhort us to fidelity in kind: "Walk worthy of the calling that you have received" (Eph 4:1).

(2) *Kletós: Called*

This is a verbal adjective. The word designates the state of accomplishing the Lord's calling, hence of being in the process of responding to God's invitation: "You are called to belong to Christ Jesus" (Rom 1:6).

Frequently, *kletós* refers specifically to a gift, an office or a responsibility: "[I], Paul, called to be an apostle" (Rom 1:1). In those instances where the reference to mission remains prominent, *kletós* continues to imply that the calling to do something presupposes a calling to be holy as God is holy. Paul addresses the members of "the Church of God in Corinth called to be saints" (1 Cor 1:2).

(3) *Epi-kaléo: To Call Upon*

This compound verb is a synonym for prayer. Having been called, the believer in turn "calls upon the name of the Lord" to be saved (Rom 10:13). Not only does the Lord's calling move us to faithful obedience and accomplishment of our mission, but also that vocation incites us to call upon God. *Epikaléo* thus completes our response to having first been called (John 15:16).

CHAPTER 6

Consecrated by God

The Lord knows us and chooses us according to God's purpose.

The Lord calls us to attain the fullness of self-identity in Christ Jesus, to do so within a certain vocational lifestyle or combination of lifestyles, and to accomplish a particular mission or constellation of missions.

The Lord also consecrates us. That is, God makes us holy by incorporating us into the inner life of the Trinity. This consecration begins in time and endures for eternity.

A prime goal of God's willing us, electing us and calling us is our individual sanctification, our personal deification. The Lord had revealed this purpose already at the time of the Levitical code:

> I am Yahweh, your God.
> Prepare yourselves to be consecrated and made holy
> because I am holy (Lev 11:44).

The New Testament reaffirms our vocation to holiness in expressions like: "Be perfect as your heavenly Father is perfect" (Matt 5:48. See Jas 1:4; 1 Pet 1:16; 1 John 3:3; etc.).

A. The Biblical Notion of Consecration

The Hebrew idea of consecration finds its origin in the verb root q-d-sh: to be holy. The New Testament authors render this concept into Greek by the adjective *hágios* and its cognates.[1]

[1]See *TDNT*, I:88–115.

(1) Qadásh: To Be Holy

The primitive meaning of q-d-sh is to divide or to separate. In a religious context q-d-sh refers to whatever is set apart for use in relation to God. In ordinary life this contrast is expressed in terms of "cultic" as distinct from "common."

Qadásh in the qal, or simple active form, means to be holy. In the niphal, or simple passive/reflexive form, it signifies to be rendered holy, to be regarded as holy, to be sanctified or reverenced. In the piel, or intensive active form, the verb means to set apart for sacred use, to hallow or sanctify, to appoint a fast or to institute a religious observance, to prepare for sacred rites; hence, to purify. In the hithpael, or intensive reflexive form, it signifies to prepare oneself before approaching the sacred, to be celebrated or to be kept holy (e.g., the Sabbath day). The hiphil, or causative active form, of qadásh means to make holy or to cause to become holy; hence, to consecrate. In the hophal, or causative passive form, it signifies to be consecrated.

Two other important words come from the root q-d-sh: qodésh, a noun meaning holiness or that which is consecrated to God, and qadósh, an adjective meaning holy or sacred. The noun, used in relation to cult, denotes a state of being rather than an action: for example, "the Holy of Holies" (Exod 26:33-34). The adjective is descriptive of God above all and thus becomes an equivalent for "divine."

The phrase "the holy name of Yahweh" in the Priestly Code (Lev 22:2) is a Hebraism stating that the very essence of the Lord is holiness. For this reason, we pray in the Our Father: "May your name be held holy" (Matt 6:9—i.e., "You are holiness itself. Enable us to experience your inner life, your holiness.").

The Lord reveals the "holy name" to the Israelites on Sinai (Exod 3:13-15) and enters into a covenant with them (Exod 24:4-8). Yahweh who is holy (i.e. utterly transcendent) and who dwells in their midst causes Israel to be a "holy people," a nation set apart (Deut 7:6; 26:19; Lev 19:2).

The prophets give qadósh a deeply spiritual meaning, and bring it into alliance with moral action. Thus, we are holy to the degree that the Lord draws us to approach the divine transcend-

ence. We witness to that consecratedness by attitudes and behavior which accord with the divine will.

The Book of Hosea presents a significant development in the
prophetic theology of consecration. God as holy contrasts with
whatever is human and creaturely (Hos 11:9). Yahweh's holiness is thus opposed to "unholy" nature. Nonetheless, the Lord's
holiness expresses itself through creative love which brings into
being, destroys and re-creates out of the ashes of defeat (Hos
6:1-3). Hosea masterfully contrasts the hurting yet tender loving
holiness of Yahweh with the profanity of God's whoring people
(Hos 4:14, 12:1). Yahweh's forgiving holy love effects conversion which opens the way for God's people to participate again
in the Lord's own holiness (Hos 14:2-10).

The holiness of God is pivotal in the theology of Isaiah. In
coming to the consciousness of his own call, the prophet encounters the thrice *qadósh* Yahweh Sabaoth (Isa 6:3). Holiness so
denotes God's innermost secret essence that it cannot be directly
revealed to mortals. What we perceive is the Lord's glory—
kabód—which "fills the earth" (Isa 6:3). Having experienced
God's glory—that is, the created manifestation of Yahweh's
uncreated *qodésh*—Isaiah realizes the extent of his inner poverty, sinfulness and mortality (Isa 6:5). Moreover, he cannot purify himself by his own initiative. Yahweh has to purge him and
thereby prepare him for his mission (Isa 6:7-9). Isaiah does not
refer to himself as holy, but he does speak of the final state of all
the redeemed as *qadósh* (Isa 4:3). Referring to Yahweh as "the
holy One of Israel" (Isa 12:6; 17:7; 29:19), Isaiah describes the
Lord as both transcendent and immanent. God as holiness itself
transforms and purifies a remnant of the people into "a holy nation" (Isa 10:21).

(2) *Hágios: Holy*

The Greek translators of the Hebrew Scriptures chose a sel-
dom used word—*hágios*—to render *qadósh*. Furthermore, the
Hebrew notion of holiness underlies the New Testament theology of *hágios*.

According to the New Testament, the Father is holy (John
17:11); Jesus is holy (Luke 1:35, 4:34); the Spirit is holy (Matt
1:18,20). The Trinity is holy, holy, holy (Rev 4:8).

The Pauline letters describe God's holiness as integral to our personhood:

> Don't you know that you are God's temple
> and that God's Spirit dwells within you? . . .
> Well then, God's temple is holy
> and you are that temple (1 Cor 3:16-17. See Eph 2:21).

Paul urges us to offer ourselves "as a living sacrifice, holy and pleasing to God" (Rom 12:1; 15:16). He exhorts: "Do not conform to the world around you, but let yourselves be transformed by the renewing of your inner selves" (Rom 12:2). A person so disposed is called a *hágion*—a holy one, a "saint" (Phil 4:21).

The norm for morality in the New Testament is not some cultic act, but a state of being which results from the indwelling Trinity. Holy behavior flows from Christocentric holiness—that is, from the life of Jesus coursing through our veins. The mere performance of rituals does not make us holy. The Lord alone directly sanctifies, and God does this from within our inner depths. Ideally, therefore, ritualization is the symbolic reenactment of that interior reality, the sacrament of that mystery. Because God is Spirit (John 4:24) and God is Love (1 John 4:16), the quintessence of our holiness and spirituality is *agápe* (Mark 12:30-31; 1 Cor 13:1-13).

(3) *Hagiázo: To Consecrate, to Sanctify*

The New Testament verb for "consecrate" is *hagiázo*. The best known passage in which this word occurs is the Lord's Prayer: "Hallowed be your name"—literally, "May your name be consecrated" (Matt 6:9; Luke 11:2). Obviously, we do not consecrate God. God sanctifies us. The Lord is consecrated by being God, and the Lord causes us to participate in that holiness. The sense of the aorist passive imperative in Matthew 6:9 becomes evident when viewed in relation to the petitions which follow it. We humans adore the Father as little as we respect his presence within us ("Your kingdom come") or allow his will to be done (Matt 6:10). It therefore behooves us to hallow him, to acknowledge the mystery of his inner life, to experience reverentially the Father's transcendent immanence.

The Father consecrates his Son from all eternity (John 10:36). Christ is thus the holy one in whom all others are sanctified (Heb 2:11). The fact that Jesus consecrates his apostles (John 17:19) and the Church (Eph 5:26-27) attests to his divinity. The Holy Spirit consecrates Paul and the Gentiles to whom he is sent (Rom 15:16). This sanctifying activity affirms the Spirit's own divinity.

Referring to the consecrated Christian, Paul ordinarily uses the passive voice—those being consecrated (1 Cor 1:2; Rom 15:16). He thereby indicates a divinely-constituted state of being. In the context of marriage, for example, Paul speaks of God effecting holiness in the nonChristian spouse through his/her Christian partner and children (1 Cor 7:14).

According to the New Testament, consecration is not static or once-and-for-all. It is ongoing:

> Let the one who is holy
>   be consecrated further (Rev 22:11).

(4) *New Testament Derivatives*

Three Greek nouns are translated by the English expressions: consecrating, consecration and consecratedness.

(a) *Hagiasmós: Consecrating.* As an action noun, *hagiasmós* is more accurately rendered by "consecrating" than "consecration." In the New Testament, we find this word only in the epistles. It accentuates the moral behavior which flows from having been sanctified. Thus, a Christian's actions are in accord with God's holy will (1 Thess 4:3-4). The Holy Spirit's activity, which effects Trinitarian life within us, is *hagiasmós* (2 Thess 2:13).

The opposite of *hagiasmós* is "uncleanness" (1 Thess 4:7). In this respect, the action noun conveys the same thought as the sixth Beatitude: "Blessed are the clean of heart" (Matt 5:8). That is, graced are they whose behavior springs from the life of God within them.

(b) *Hagiótes: Consecration.* The previous word, *hagiasmós*, denotes moral behavior in accord with the process of being made holy. *Hagiótes*, on the other hand, denotes an interior disposition, the state which follows upon having been made holy (2 Cor 1:12).

Holiness is the most essential of the divine attributes. Yet, the Lord calls us to participate in that very holiness. God prepares us for this participation by painstakingly disciplining us (Heb 12:10).

(c) *Hagiosúne: Consecratedness.* Rather than moral behavior or a state of being, *hagiosúne* designates an essential quality of both God and the Christian being transformed in God.[2]

In his prologue to Romans (1:4), Paul uses this word to describe what we would call today the divine nature of Christ. In 2 Corinthians 7:1, the noun describes a human quality—our personal participation in the divine nature, hence, our deification or divinization: "Let us cleanse ourselves from all contamination of flesh and spirit, thereby perfecting our consecratedness in the worship of God." The participle "perfecting" indicates a gradual process in which we voluntarily cooperate with God's initiative.

B. Two English Verbs: To Consecrate and to Sanctify

Even though in English the verbs "to consecrate" and "to sanctify" are sometimes used interchangeably, they do have different nuances.

To consecrate is said of both persons and things. A person can, for example, consecrate him/herself to God by making vows. We can also consecrate an altar, a chalice or a church edifice, although today we tend to use the word "bless" in these instances. In either case, the intent is to reserve for sacred use, to set someone or something apart for God.

In reference to things other than the sacraments, to consecrate or to bless does not effect an interior change. Consecration does not render them intrinsically holy, but rather separates them from their ordinary usages.

In reference to persons, however, to consecrate or to be consecrated always suggests a radical interior change. When people consecrate themselves to the Lord, they do so because God has first consecrated them. Vows, promises, etc. are therefore, responses to an interior calling. They are the external signs of an

[2]See *Contemplation*, 13–20; *Spiritual Direction*, 15–32.

already existing internal grace. If the interior vocation is not present and operative, the sign symbolizes nothing.

The word "consecrate" refers also to the Eucharist. At the consecration of the Mass, bread and wine become sacramentally the Body and Blood of Christ.

Although to consecrate can be said of both persons and things, to sanctify is predicated only of people. Moreover, both we and God can set somebody or something aside for sacred use, but only the Lord can actually sanctify someone. To sanctify means not only to declare holy, but also to make intrinsically holy. Sanctification refers to a radical change which the indwelling Trinity effects within a person.

To sanctify means to deify, to divinize. To be sanctified is to be transformed in God by God.

CHAPTER 7

Consecrated unto God

The Lord consecrates us for a reason: to transform us, to deify us. Personal holiness, therefore, remains a divinely ordained goal of every human life.

A. The Universal Call to Holiness

The Lord calling us each by our own name and destining us to divinization makes us specially chosen and beloved. By calling us, the Lord sets us apart for God. Thus, the Lord consecrates us. What we name "vocation" is the milieu in which and the way through which we become holy as God is holy (Lev 19:2; Matt 5:48).

Yet, the Lord does not call and consecrate only a select few. God calls all persons by their individual names and consecrates each one to participate in the inner life of the Trinity.

Both Scripture and tradition attest to the universal call to holiness: "[All of you], return to me with your whole heart" (Joel 2:12). "As the one who called [all of] you is holy, so you must also become holy" (1 Pet 1:15). "Jesus preached holiness to each and every one of his disciples, regardless of their state in life: 'Be perfect as your heavenly Father is perfect' (Matt 5:48)."[1]

Applied to God, the term "holiness" stresses two divine characteristics: (1) It denotes the Lord's innermost essence which is ineffable, mysterious, divine, transcendent, incomprehen-

[1] "Dogmatic Constitution on the Church," *The Documents of Vatican II*, 40. See *Contemplation*, 13–20.

sible—God's absolute otherness in relation to creation. (2) It connotes also the unconditional love, the immanence, the ever-abiding presence of the Lord in relation to the elect.

The holiness of God being reproduced within us causes a twofold effect: (1) It progressively transforms us into the likeness of Christ (Rom 8:29), and (2) it gradually purifies our hearts of all immaturity, sinfulness and egocentricity (John 15:1-4).

The universal call to holiness then is God's irresistible invitation to all people of all times to enter into an everlasting personal relationship of love with the Trinity. Since the Lord is the source of all holiness, our holiness is in effect a participation in the very being of God. It is the gift to us of communion in divine life.

Therefore, this call is not primarily to some-thing, whether that be happiness, joy, peace or fulfillment. It remains preeminently a call to interpersonal communion with some-One—God, in whom we find our happiness, joy, peace and fulfillment. Our response must be the commitment in faith, hope and love of our deepest selves to Father, Son and Spirit who have first offered themselves to us in love. The mutual surrender integral to call and response is such that God and the human person indwell each other (John 14-17). Our will and God's will ultimately become one. In the resurrection we become God in participant transformation.

The universal call to holiness in which we all participate by reason of our existence is the foundation of the widespread belief in the universality of revelation and of salvation. Since the beginning of time and in a multitude of ways, God has revealed something of the divine purpose to all peoples—even to the most primitive—so that they can in their own manner respond knowingly and voluntarily to God's loving initiative (Rom 1:19-20, 8:19-25). Many people believe that besides willing the salvation of all, God actually does save each and every one (Isa 55:10-11; Rom 8:28-39).

Jesus died not only for all. He died specifically for each one. Not only is there a universal call to holiness, but also there exists a particular calling for each individual. Our vocation not only directs us toward consummate transformation in God, but also our calling is the contemporary context of our ongoing transformation and purification.

Jesus says: "You are clean already by means of the word I have spoken to you" (John 15:3). That "word" is our vocation. That word is his call which converts, sanctifies and draws us to himself. His word—our vocation—is the context within which our personal transformation transpires.

B. The Particular Calling of Each Person

While the call to holiness is universal, God nonetheless calls each individual to a particular *self-identity* in Christ Jesus, to a specific vocational *lifestyle* and to a special *mission*. The Lord gifts everyone with a unique personhood. God calls each to become his/her true self through some way of life. God sends each individual forth to contribute in a unique manner to the building up of the Body of Christ (Eph 4:12).

(1) *The Example of Jeremiah*

We find many instances of callings in both the Hebrew Scriptures and the New Testament. One of the most graphic and theologically insightful is the call of Jeremiah (Jer 1:4-19).

Jeremiah formulated the description of his vocation probably late in life. The passage seems to be a synthesis of his life-long struggle to come to grips with his vocation. It explicates what he eventually realized was Yahweh's calling for him to be, to become and to do. However, in addition to his personal experience, Jeremiah's vocational reflection embodies certain truths common to the way in which God calls many, if not most, people.

The prophet opens the account by placing the following words on the lips of Yahweh:

> Before forming you in the womb,
>   I knew you.
> Before bringing you to birth,
>   I consecrated you.
> I [had already] sent you forth
>   as prophet to the nations (Jer 1:5).

In the Hebrew, the expression "I knew you" indicates completed action on God's part. For Jeremiah, however, God knowing him meant a process of painstaking growth. The description of Yahweh's act of knowing Jeremiah as already accomplished emphasizes God's steadfast resolve to bring to completion the work which would extend over Jeremiah's entire earthly sojourn.

The Lord resolves also to accomplish throughout the course of our lives the work begun at the moment of our individual creation. By knowing us, God brings us into being in such a way that we are becoming. Thus, our existence and our vocation are not static but dynamic. They are bestowed not all-in-one-fellswoop but in an evolving manner. Even before forming us, God knows us in such a way that we receive the impetus to reach maximum individuation and consummate transformation. Paradoxically, we are and we are not. We are, because we exist. Yet, we still are not all that we are to become.

For the Lord, to know us is to experience us in every fiber of our being-becoming. The Psalmist poignantly captures this truth:

> Yahweh, you probe me and you know me.
> You know when I sit and when I stand . . .
> Whether I walk or lie down,
>   you are there.
> You know every detail of my conduct.
> The word is not yet on my tongue, Yahweh,
>   and you already know the whole of it . . .
> You created my inmost being.
> You knit me together in my mother's womb.
> You know me through and through (Ps 139:1-4, 13-15).

God's knowing and caring elicit our response. Because the Lord knows us in divine love, we are enabled to become holy as God is holy (Lev 19:2; Matt 5:48). Thus, Yahweh reveals to Jeremiah: "I consecrated you" (Jer 1:5). That is, "I am causing you to become sanctified, to participate in my own life." In so enabling us, God implants within the depths of our being an irresistible longing for fullness of life.

As we saw in the previous chapter, the original Hebrew meaning of "to make holy" was to distinguish, to separate, to divide, to contrast. When applied to Creator and creatures, this distinction was translated into "divine" and "human," with emphasis on the infinite gulf between the two. When applied to worship, this separation signified "sacred" as set off from "profane." When applied to ordinary life, this division meant "cultic" as opposed to "common." When applied to behavior, this variance contrasted "clean" and "unclean," "pure" and "impure."

The New Testament preserved the spirit of those Hebrew differences, while catapulting the ultimate meaning of holiness into the inner life of the Trinity. Thus, divine holiness is not only that which separates us from God, but also in virtue of the incarnation that into which we are being transformed.

In the light of Judeo-Christian revelation, therefore, holiness separates us not from our creatureliness or our humanity, but rather from our immaturities, sinfulness and egocentrism. Ultimately, our participation in God's holiness divides us from our fleshiness (Rom 7:14) and mortality (1 Cor 15:44), so that we can partake of the fullness (Eph 1:23; 3:19) of transforming union.[2]

As Jeremiah emphasizes, there never had been a moment in his existence when God was not knowing him and consecrating him. So too it is with us. There has never been a time in our personal salvation history when we were not children of God, when God was not forming us in the divine likeness, when the Lord was not calling us by our very own name.

How then might we conceive the relationship of the gift of our personal being-becoming to that of our mission?

We find basically two static and extremely anthropomorphic theories which predicate successive acts on God's part. First, the Lord has a specific task to be accomplished. Therefore, God brings into being a particular person for that purpose. It is as if God were to ask: "Who am I going to create in order to fulfill this objective?" The second theory postulates that the Lord brings a person into existence, then searches about to discover or to invent a mission for him/her: "Now that I have created you, what am I going to do with you?" Both theories are grossly simplistic. Moreover, they arise from asking the wrong question: "Which comes first—the person or the mission?"

The theology of vocation implicit in Jeremiah 1:4-19 does

[2]See *Spiritual Direction*, 15–32.

not accord with those two approaches. Rather, Jeremiah's experience is this: In the initial act of bringing the prophet into being, God set in motion the thrust of who Jeremiah was to be, how he was to become and what he was to do. Applying that insight to ourselves, we can say that from the womb God not only endows our self-identity with a general direction, but also gifts many people with a vocation to a certain lifestyle and to some mission. The Lord effects all this simultaneously with the bestowal of our individual personhood.

Grammatically, Jeremiah 1:5 describes Yahweh's formative activity before birth as incomplete. It is moving toward accomplishment. God began to create and to form Jeremiah in his mother's womb, but it took a lifetime to complete that work. We are like Jeremiah in this respect too. God's creation and formation of us are an ongoing process. The Lord sets in motion the thrust of our call in the initial act of individual creation. However, the Lord unfolds, reveals and actualizes this innate direction only gradually throughout the course of our lives.

The matrix of this formation is our personhood in all its actuality: maturity and sinfulness, harmony and conflict, joys and sufferings, successes and failures, hopes and disappointments. God works both directly from within us and indirectly through all the converging circumstances of our daily life—employment, ministry, relationships, leisure, etc. The Father is continuously creating and re-creating us in the image of his Son.

> We know that for those who love God,
>   God works with them in all things for good.
> These have been called according the the Lord's purpose
>   (Rom 8:28).

(2) Call, Calling and Discernment

If there is a difference between the two words "call" and "calling," it consists in this: Call can be understood in a static once-and-for-all sense, while calling evokes ongoing progressive activity.

We do not respond like robots to the vocational thrust which we receive at our inception. Being-becoming, calling to some lifestyle and missioning are gifts bestowed in the raw. We work with God in developing them over the entire span of our earthly sojourn. They evolve and our consciousness of them develops. We remain always interacting, interrelating and co-creating with the Lord in every detail of our lives.[3]

It is the indwelling Trinity who bestows our threefold vocational thrust—our who, how and what—either with our inception or at some other point in our salvation history. This truth contains the key to all vocational discernment. Our basic spiritual direction is within us.[4] Therefore, vocational discernment must correlate with our personal faith experience—the experience of God within us and of our growth in the Lord. We remain forever accountable to that innate thrust, and only by fidelity to it do we attain the "peace which the world cannot give" (John 14:27).

GOD'S DEVELOPING CALL

CHAPTER 8

Christian Vocational Lifestyles

As the biblical authors put it: Willing us to exist, God knows us and chooses us to be. Having chosen us, the Lord calls us each by name and consecrates us. That choosing, calling and consecrating we term "our vocation."

Our vocation is both eternal and temporal. It is eternal because even before forming us in the womb the Lord had already consecrated us (Jer 1:5). Moreover, our eternity will consist in the everlasting realization of that consecration—unending, ever-deepening communion with Father, Son and Spirit. Our vocation is also temporal because it unfolds in space and time. It extends from the moment of inception to the instant of death.[1] Thus, we experience a vocation within a vocation—a temporal particular calling within an eternal universal call to holiness.

In several respects, our eternal vocation corresponds to *who* the Lord is calling us to be. Who we are destined to be are unique persons transformed in God by God. Who we have been foreknown, chosen and called to be are singular individuals deified and divinized by participation in the life of the Trinity. This self-identity and transformation begin with inception and develop slowly throughout our earthly sojourn.[2]

Our temporal vocation, on the other hand, corresponds primarily to *how* that spiritual journey unfolds in the here and now as well as to *what* we do for God and for others. How we become

[1]See *Spiritual Journey,* 19–21, 42–45.
[2]See Ibid. 39–52.

is distinguishable from what we are commissioned to do. "How" refers to vocational lifestyle. "What" refers to ministry, apostolate or mission in this life.

A. The Notion of Vocational Lifestyle

In contemporary English, "lifestyle" refers to an individual's typical way of living. People speak of "the lifestyle of the rich and famous," "hippie lifestyle," "degenerate lifestyle," etc. Because of these common or pejorative associations, some persons object to using the term in relation to Christian vocation. Others deem that "style" is too weak a noun to express the mystery of calling. We admit validity in both objections. We do use several turns of speech to describe this aspect of calling, for instance: "way of life," "mode of living," "manner of becoming." Nonetheless, while recognizing its limitations, we have a certain preference for the word "lifestyle."

In reference to vocation, our understanding of the term "lifestyle" is specific and restricted. *Life* bespeaks that life which God has given us and the fullness of life to which the Lord has destined us. This life is from God, to God and completely sustained by God. *Style* indicates mode, manner, way of actualizing that life. *Lifestyle* then is a compound word which indicates the junction where our *zoé* (the life by which we live; God's life in us— John 10:10; 14:6) merges with our *bíos* (the life which we live; our mortal life—1 Tim 2:2).[3]

There are many lifestyles which can legitimately be called Christian. In this book we accentuate three such vocations: marriage, celibacy and singlehood.[4] Each one constitutes a relatively self-contained calling.

By "self-contained" we mean that the basic elements of a particular mode of living are sufficient for holistic personal growth. An authentic celibate, for instance, attains fulfillment primarily through solitude, community and some ministry.

[3]See *TDNT*, II:832–872.

[4]Other vocational lifestyles could be mentioned, for example: the religious life, the monastic life, the apostolic life, the contemplative life, the eremitical life. And there are still others: different forms of communes, like an Israeli kibbutz; various kinds of ashrams, whether Christian or Hindu; etc.

S/he does not need a spouse and children to experience wholeness of being. However, we qualify "self-contained" with "relatively" because not one of these three vocational lifestyles exists alone. Each of them compenetrates and coexists with at least one other. Most married, celibate and single persons, for instance, are called also to some form of the apostolic life.

A vocational lifestyle in the strict sense entails more than a vague thrust toward a certain way of Christian living. For example, an authentic calling to marriage cannot be complete until the person experiences a vocation to marry someone in particular. Two people receive not only a general calling to the conjugal life, but also a specific vocation to marry each other.

A vocational lifestyle involves a fundamental way of becoming our true selves and of relating to others. It is an all-embracing, all-penetrating mode of living, of thinking about ourselves and of interacting with others.

Our vocational "how" is all-embracing, because every facet of our daily existence falls within the parameters of its influence. It extends meaning and relevance to every aspect of our life. How God calls us to live, as well as how we respond to that vocation, directly affects our ups and downs, our likes and dislikes, our hopes and fears, our present and future.

Our vocational lifestyle is all-penetrating too. If I am married, for instance, the reality of the conjugal "we-us" permeates all aspects of my life. The covenant between my spouse and myself impacts every pain and joy, every hesitation and decision of my concrete existence.

Our vocational "how" contributes immeasurably to our self-identity and self-awareness. God has destined us to a transformation which we cannot begin to imagine (1 Cor 2:9). The depth of our inner poverty is so far beyond our comprehension that it leaves us reeling (Rom 7:21). Yet, through our lifestyle we receive increasing insight into who we are and how we are to become our true self in God.

Our vocational lifestyle determines to a large degree our rapport with others. If I am single, for instance, I may date several people. However, if I am married or celibate and wish to remain faithful to my calling, I will not be available for dating—even should I take someone out for lunch, for a stroll in the park, for a walk along the beach.

Because of who we are and how we are becoming, we make certain choices. If we were different, we would have to opt another way. Our mode of living is to a large degree an extension of ourselves. Who we are precedes how we live and what we do. Yet, our God-willed lifestyle also radically influences our personhood.

Ask a woman, for example: "Who are you?" She may reply: "Mrs. Jane Brown Smith." That is: "I am Jane Brown, wife of John Smith." Her marital vocation directly qualifies who she is. Similarly, Jane's husband, by virtue of their marriage, is no longer simply an "I." He has become, by reason of their mutual vocational lifestyle, a "we" (Matt 19:6). His wife is not his, but to him and with him. She is not a possession, but a gift and an equal partner in a covenant. His interior and exterior being is specified by Jane and her world. He chooses his employment and ministry in relation to their common vocational lifestyle. What he does or does not do with his leisure flows out of how he and she are becoming. His married life modifies his rapport with all other women, including his mother (Gen 2:24; Matt 19:5). His physical dwelling, his living habits, the car he drives, the company he keeps all possess a relatedness to her. Marriage radically changes his decision-making process. Who is he? He is John Smith, husband of Jane Brown.

The Gospel according to Mark presents an interesting insight into the disciples' evolving consciousness of the self-identity of Jesus and his way of life. Mark accentuates two decisive questions in the course of his sixteen-chapter narrative. First, on the lips of a myriad of people he puts the question, either expressed or implied: "Who is this man?" Peter eventually proclaims: "You are the Christ" (Mark 8:29). Then, from that threshold at Caesarea Philippi the pivotal issue becomes: "Who is the Christ?" Jesus proceeds to reveal the authentic Messiah. This revelation reaches its climax on Calvary when the Roman centurian confesses his divinity: "Truly, this man was the Son of God" (Mark 15:39). Thus, the revelation of who Jesus is in Mark goes from "this man" to "the Christ" to "the Son of God." *Who*, then, is Jesus? He is the Christ, the God-man. *How*, therefore, is

Jesus? His self-identity developed in the context of his becoming fully human, while remaining truly God. His lifestyle was that of the theandric Christ, unique in all salvation history.

The mysterious reality of the Christ-event does not easily fit into human categories. Nonetheless, most people would say that Jesus was celibate. Certainly, he was not married, and he was other than single. Surely his mission was beyond anything that we can conceptualize. The vocational "who," "how" and "what" of Jesus dovetail into one: the "Word made flesh" (John 1:14); "the Christ, the Son of the living God" (Matt 16:16); "the Lord" (1 Cor 12:3). Our vocational lifestyles and missions, however, are distinguishable, even though they remain deeply integrated with our personal development.

Our vocational lifestyle then is a dynamic gift from God. It is to us, yet not of us. It is for us, but not a possession to do with as we please. Our lifestyle specifies our way of becoming both within ourselves and in relation to others. It radically influences our self-perception as well as our rapport with our evolving self, with other persons and with the diverse situations around us. It must be nurtured, challenged and let go when the time is ripe to move on. Our lifestyle is always ongoing, constantly developing, increasingly Christogenic.[5]

Thus, as far as our vocational "how" is concerned, we never have it made. Our Christian lifestyle unfolds to us as well as with us.

B. Three "Basic" Vocational Lifestyles

We speak of the vocational lifestyles of marriage, celibacy and singlehood as "basic" in three senses:

(1) These distinct callings serve as foundations to other ways of living and acting. Not only do these modes of becoming coexist with other vocational lifestyles, but also in relation to these others they act as does a base to the rest of an edifice.

(2) Ordinarily, each of these three remains exclusive of the other two. Usually, we do not find the same individual simultaneously married and single, married and celibate or single and celibate.

[5]As in "Christogenesis." See *Receptivity*, 10–11; *Spiritual Journey*, 19–20.

(3) These basic modes of living are all-inclusive in the sense that each spiritually adult Christian is either married, celibate or single.

The vocational lifestyles of marriage and celibacy are analogous to the outermost rays of a spectrum. Singlehood would then be like the middle. We all start off single. Most marry. Many remain single. A few become celibate. Just as multiple shades of color exist within the spectrum and blend imperceptibly one into the other, so too there are variations within and overlappings among these lifestyles.

While God does not ordinarily call a person to two basic vocational lifestyles at the same time, we discover in the history of spirituality certain unique situations:

(1) We find instances of "virginal marriages." Catholic tradition believes that such was the case between Mary and Joseph. The supposition is that their marriage and others like theirs are not consummated because of Christ and the gospel. We would, however, term the lifestyle of these persons "married" rather than "celibate" because they continue living together in an all-embracing and all-penetrating spousal, though non-genital, relationship.

(2) Examples of nonconsummated marriages exist in which sexual intercourse does not occur for reasons of illness, impotency or a choice other than Christ and the gospel. People in such marriages may or may not engage in erotic love expressions, and may or may not live in close spousal intimacy.

(3) There are also a few instances of marriages in which sexual intercourse occurs for a while, but at a certain point both spouses agree out of a sense of calling to cease all genital expression of their love. In some of these cases, the cessation is only temporary. In other marriages, it endures for the rest of their wedded life. However long it lasts, the couple remain married, but engage in a sort of eschatological living out of their marriage. For this direction to be an authentic vocation, both spouses must simultaneously experience the same calling.

When the genital expression of love has not existed at all or at some point ceases in a marriage as a result of an authentic vocation, some people refer to this living together as "celibate marriage." In reality, however, the couple's basic lifestyle remains more married than celibate. There is much more to married life—as an all-embracing and all-penetrating mode of interacting—than sexual intercourse. Conversely, celibacy consists of much more than abstinence from erotic expression of love.

The cessation of genital intimacy occurs in some marriages due to factors such as boredom, alienation or irreconcilable differences. Some couples in this situation continue to live under the same roof, while going their separate ways. In effect, this option smacks more of single rather than married life.

When medical considerations cause husbands and wives to terminate the genital expression of their love, many of these couples remain far more married than either celibate or single in their basic lifestyle. In these cases, interpersonal intimacy and conjugal covenant are not affected adversely by the medical factor.

Reflecting for a moment on the few considerations above, the reader can begin to appreciate how complicated any discussion of specific vocational lifestyles becomes. It is often very difficult to discern in the concrete where one lifestyle leaves off and another begins. Yet, this ambiguity need not stop us from trying to understand more deeply the faith dimension underlying vocational discernment and commitment.

We speak, therefore, of marriage, celibacy and singlehood not as clear-cut categories or parallel lines. Rather, we see them as accents which contain a certain ebb and flow of innumerable and inscrutable forms of actualization.

C. Similarities and Differences Among These Lifestyles

Marriage, celibacy and singlehood as Christian vocations have this in common: Each postulates its own spiritual imperative. Spouses, celibates, single persons experience from within themselves the following truth: "I can become myself transformed in God only by freely embracing my particular calling."

As a Christian vocation, marriage is a formally vowed lifestyle. Persons living the celibate life also ordinarily take vows, although not necessarily in a publicly professed fashion. The single life is not usually vowed. However, all three lifestyles—as Christian modes of becoming—are equally committed ways of living. They are authentic callings on equal footing before God. None is better in itself than another. One is "better" only for the person whom God so calls.

In marriage, each spouse vows in love to the other the sharing of this earthly existence. In celibacy, the person vows, promises or dedicates in love his/her mortal life to Christ. In singlehood, persons live the single life for some time, and at a certain point some choose positively to remain single.

God transforms two spouses both directly One-to-one and indirectly through each other and through their marital covenant. The Lord transforms a celibate both directly One-to-one and indirectly through relationships and the celibate life itself. God transforms a single person both directly One-to-one and indirectly through relationships and the single life itself.

The various ministries to which God sends married, celibate and single persons are also effective instruments for their personal divinization. Vocational lifestyles and ministerial pursuits interrelate to form a multifaceted but integrated vocation.

All three basic vocational lifestyles entail a consecration on the Lord's part, because through each of them God makes the person holy. Marriage and celibacy also necessarily evoke from those so called a personal consecration. Spouses consecrate themselves to each other and together they consecrate their marriage to God. A celibate, by definition, has consecrated him/herself and his/her life directly to God. Single persons, by vocation, are not usually consecrated to God in either of the above two ways, although they remain consecrated by God.

When people pray "for vocations," most think spontaneously of "the priesthood" and "the religious life." The presbyteral office, strictly speaking, is a ministry—a vocational *what* to which God calls a few. Moreover, there can exist within that calling a variety of further vocational refinements: missionary, pastor, prison chaplain, etc. A priest may or may not be a personally consecrated celibate. Interiorly, some priests are in reality more "single" than celibate. Experience proves also that a few priests are in fact more "married" than single. The religious life, on the other hand, is properly speaking a vocational *how*, with consecrated celibacy at its core. As a specific lifestyle, the religious life consists of a celibate calling combined with a vocation to some other lifestyle, for example: apostolic or contemplative life, monastic or eremitical life.

CHAPTER 9

Dawning Light

Our vocation—not only in the sense of who we are called to be, but also for many persons in terms of lifestyle and mission—begins when we begin. It is integral to our initial act of existence. Yet, God's calling is not fully formed from the outset. It is like a seed which takes root, grows and only eventually becomes full-blown. The flowering of our vocation requires time, discipline and incredibly intricate interaction among ourselves, God and the world around us. Moreover, the Lord does not impose a calling on us. God rather elicits our free response in such a way that we remain co-workers (1 Cor 3:9) and active collaborators with God on our spiritual journey.

Our vocation itself develops and our consciousness of that calling likewise evolves. For the remainder of this book, we examine that twofold maturation process as it is influenced by a myriad of factors.

A. An Individual's Vocation and the Callings of Other People

The unfolding of our vocation occurs amid intimate relatedness not only with God but also with others. Vocation develops within a communal setting. While the Lord calls each of us to a specific self-identity, a lifestyle and a mission, God is also calling every person who influences our spiritual journey to his/her own vocational who, how and what. Many of those vocations interconnect and converge upon one another, forming an unbelievably complex network:

> The life and death of every one of us
> influences someone else (Rom 14:7).

The Spirit moves this convoluted web of interacting vocations toward fulfillment in the person of Jesus (Gal 4:4-7). This historical situation unfolds according to the Father's plan for the cosmos (Rom 8:22) which is twofold: that "God become all in all" (1 Cor 15:28) and that the whole of creation be recapitulated in Christ (Col 1:15-20).

Each person's vocation to a Christian lifestyle remains unique. Nonetheless, among individual vocations to the same way of life common characteristics and patterns are distinguishable. These commonalities provide the basis for vocational discernment. There are, for example, distinct signs which indicate a calling to marriage rather than to celibacy or singlehood.

B. Vocation, Desire and Consciousness

From a faith perspective, the bestowal of a vocation, its subsequent development and the emerging consciousness of it follow this sequence in many people:

Initially, God gifts us with a vocation. Since we are literally in the womb, we receive this calling without specifically choosing it.

Then, out of that ontological reality gradually evolves a desire for the direction indicated by our vocation. We want what accords with our innate sense of meaningfulness. Hence, we spontaneously make options according to who we are called to be, how we are meant to become and what we are destined to do. Many of those choices are prereflective.

Finally, with more maturity we begin reflecting on those options. We realize that our choices in many situations have arisen out of a vocational direction which we have been pursuing from as far back as we can remember. This reflective awareness constitutes the dawning of the light which has been within us since our individual creation.

Thus, distinctions exist between our vocation, our desire for it and our consciousness of both that calling and that desire. Vocation is ontological. It is within us, but not from us. Desire is spontaneous—almost instinctual—and with the eventual introduction of awareness it becomes voluntary. Consciousness is reflective, hence, mental and cognitive.

All three of those elements evolve. Our vocation develops from our inception to death. At least in terms of self-identity, our desire to pursue who we are meant to be begins to assert itself in subtle primitive expressions shortly after birth, if not already in the womb. That desire can attain sensorimotor expressions in infancy.

Once meaningful reflection occurs, however, vocational consciousness in a more advanced form becomes possible. Vocational consciousness, properly speaking, means that we have come to recognize what we had desired spontaneously all along. We become aware of the existence of not only that desire, but also to some degree its content and source. Thus, we value that vocational desire as indicative of what God wills for us and of us.

Vocational consciousness, therefore, completes the cycle (1) of the Lord's willing and calling, (2) of our being set in motion toward God, and (3) of our reaching awareness of the Lord's calling. At this point, voluntariness bursts forth in earnest. Once we are aware of our vocation and of our personal history already proceeding in that direction, we can then begin to commit ourselves to God. With increasingly enlightened faith we can assent to and deliberately foster our self-identity, vocational lifestyle and mission. From this threshold on, an ever intensifying dialectic of vocational maturity on all levels—ontological, volitional and reflective—characterizes our spiritual journey.

Let us look more closely, first, at vocational consciousness itself and, then, from a phenomenological perspective at our spontaneous desires whether prereflective or concomitant with reflection.

C. Vocational Consciousness

The word "consciousness" in a theological context denotes the awareness, insight, enlightenment and knowledge which arise from the experience of ourselves in relation to God and creation. Consciousness comprises sensation, emotion, imagination, volition and thought. It refers to what we intuitively or cognitively perceive of ourselves and others, in contrast to what lies beyond our grasp. The adjective "vocational" refers to the Lord's calling of an individual to transformation in God and to the Lord's bestowal of the means to that end.

Thus, the phrase "vocational consciousness" bespeaks our experiential awareness of God's call emanating from within us and drawing us beyond ourselves. The phrase implies also our voluntary self-commitment to the Lord in response to that calling.

Discovery of our vocation is integral to self-discovery. Just as our self-knowledge increases gradually, so too do we attain vocational consciousness through a slow awakening. Nonetheless, the catalyst for both discoveries—that of ourselves and that of our vocation—is in many instances a radically new experience of God.[1]

The call of Isaiah (Isa 6:1-13) affords insight into the inter-relationship of a new experience of God, self-discovery and a discovery of vocation. First of all, the prophet experienced a profound awakening regarding the transcendence of Yahweh (vv. 1-4). That awakening in turn revealed to him the terrifying depths of his inner poverty (v. 5). Then, Isaiah experienced the immanence of God directly purifying him (v. 7). That purification enabled him, finally, to respond wholeheartedly to being sent forth (vv. 8-13).

Isaiah's account of his calling accentuates two of the three fundamental aspects of vocation: self-identity and mission. Each arises out of the experience of complementary qualities in God: the Lord's transcendent inner life, on the one hand, and Yahweh Sabaoth's immanent caring for the prophet and the people, on the other. Thus, integral to *who* the Lord was calling Isaiah *to be* was the truth of his "lostness" and the fact that he was "a man of unclean lips living among a people of unclean lips" (v. 5). Moreover, integral to *what* the Lord was calling the prophet *to do* was his need to be purged (vv. 8-13).

[1] See *Spiritual Journey,* 55–95, esp. 59–61.

From the womb to the tomb, God ekes out of us an ever more committed "yes" from an ever deeper level of consciousness. That "yes" emerges through moments of joyful surrender to God, as well as through moments of sin and weakness. It arises through elation and pain, insight and confusion, success and failure. As we mature spiritually, our faith perspective toward our self-identity, lifestyle and mission becomes more qualitative. That deepening faith enlightens us with increasing understanding and appreciation of the mystery of our calling.

In the course of day-to-day interactions, few people give so much as a passing glance at the vocational dimension of their life. Much less do they advert to the distinctions between self-identity, lifestyle and mission. The reality of vocation is so complex and our consciousness usually so absorbed in the nitty-gritty of daily existence that such considerations rarely present themselves. Most people choose and act spontaneously, compulsively or for eminently practical reasons. Only afterwards may they reflect on the vocational sources and appropriateness of their choices. When they do reflect, however, two of the most readily observable elements in their choosing are these: prolonged consistent desire and insights derived from ordinary occurrences.

D. Prolonged Consistent Desire

Many people notice the first glimmers of a calling to a specific lifestyle already in childhood. Some persons do not recognize these proddings until adolescence or early adulthood. Others note stirrings of a vocation to marriage, singlehood or celibacy only later in life.

Usually, the first perceptions of a calling to a basic vocational lifestyle consist in a nebulous leaning in a certain direction. At the outset, this vague attraction is without specific form or forethought. We feel an inclination, but without especially adverting to it. The inclination is untested and not necessarily viewed in terms of choice or commitment. Our vocation at this stage is still fundamentally preconscious and prereflective.

As we mature, so too does our perception of God's calling. Gradually, our innate bent becomes in faith more explicit. It eventually reaches a point of urgency. However, even then we may experience periods when our calling seems to fade from consciousness for a while or when we try to reject, repress or deny it outrightly. Feelings of bewilderment, hesitation and fear may accompany our awareness of an urgency to move forward in a direction that is in us but mysteriously not of us. In and through all these responses a basic leaning persists.

Regarding a possible call to celibacy, for instance, the specifically celibate dimension of the calling is not always immediately apparent. Often, a ministry to which celibacy is attached initially attracts people to this way of life, for example: being a Pastor, a missionary Sister or a teaching Brother. These people are aware that priests and religious profess celibacy. But rarely do they advert to the fact that celibacy is a vocational lifestyle in its own right, and hence, must be chosen out of a sense of personal calling.

Formation personnel and spiritual directors need to appreciate how crucial it is for aspirants to choose celibacy as a specific vocation, independent of, though not necessarily separate from, the ministerial dimension of their calling. Both celibacy and marriage remain vocational lifestyles in their own right. They are not just appendices or conditions related to some mission, for instance, priesthood or parenting.

As we discern our individual calling more explicitly, our outlook toward that vocational lifestyle also changes. At first, a certain lack of personal involvement may characterize our attitude. We view marriage, for example, as an appealing possibility, a viable alternative to singlehood. As such, we see it as somewhat apart from ourselves, something which we could take or leave without harming our overall development. With more experience, however, our outlook grows increasingly interior. It dawns on us that the attraction toward the conjugal life arises from deep within us. Later, we come to realize that the impulse indicates an essential element of how we are to become more spiritual. Finally, we experience it as the way of life which we must choose in order to be true to ourselves and to God within us.

Not only does our consciousness of a possible vocation to marriage or celibacy evolve, but so also does our attraction. What was originally a faint interest develops gradually into eager longing. More and more urgently a certain direction imposes itself from within us. Yet, this imperative does not inflict violence, for we freely choose it and deliberately foster its development.

The evolution of the realization of a possible vocation to singlehood is generally much slower and less defined than in the case of marriage and celibacy. Usually, it expresses itself for a long time in terms of "neither marriage nor celibacy, therefore single." One may be single for quite a while before opting to remain so out of a sense of vocation.

Thus, perception of a vocation to marriage, celibacy or singlehood ordinarily takes the form of a recurring attraction toward one of the three. Provided that the source of the attraction is God, that leaning becomes with time more identifiable, until at last we experience it in faith as the direction we must pursue.

That prolonged desire constitutes an important positive sign of authenticity. Yet, the absence of a long-term attraction is not necessarily a counterindication. We cannot conclude that lack of desire for a certain lifestyle at a given point in our journey automatically excludes a possible calling in that direction later. Moreover, a superficial or egocentric attraction for one lifestyle does not necessarily mean that God is calling us to it.

If we experience absence of attraction, it is often useful to explore the source of the disinterest. For example:

With regard to marriage, does the hesitation arise principally from unresolved negative experiences or attitudes? An unhappy relationship between our parents, absence of a positive model of wedded life, paralyzing fear of commitment, sexual dysfunction or frigidity can cause considerable hesitancy. Or, does the disinclination toward the conjugal life spring primarily from a positive desire for the creative independence of singlehood? This latter could be from God even when unresolved negative experiences regarding marriage persist.

With respect to celibacy, does the disinclination arise from an impression that celibate life is barren or empty? Have we formed a negative attitude toward celibacy because we see inauthenticity and lack of integrity in some persons who profess it? Or, is our disinclination the consequence of a sense of vocation to marriage or to the single life? The reticence to embrace a celibate lifestyle can spring from a combination of positive and negative factors, as in the case of marriage or singlehood. The function of discernment is to search for God's movement amid all those influences. The purpose of pursuing self-knowledge is to discover ways to mitigate the impact of the negative factors.

Sometimes people find themselves in the position of experiencing no attraction to either marriage or celibacy. In these instances, it may be that a calling to one or the other has not yet sufficiently exerted its influence upon their consciousness. It could also be that the Lord has other designs for these individuals. They may be called to the single life.

E. Ordinary Occurrences as Indicators of Vocational Direction

Throughout the process of maturation many situations related to day-to-day living afford insight into the possibility of a calling to marriage, celibacy or singlehood. For example:

(1) *Childhood and Adolescent Fantasies*

The manner in which we spontaneously imagine ourselves in the future often flows out of the preconscious thrust of our becoming. Fantasizing—whether awake or in dreams—is frequently a significant indicator of unconscious activity. This is especially true when we conjure up a consistent and recurrent image.

A girl may frequently play mother or nun, business executive or doctor, etc. A boy may act out the role of father, priest, policeman or teacher, etc. Either may imagine him/herself as a world traveler or as a lone missionary among a foreign people.

(2) *Manner of Dating*

Adolescent dating awakens a boy to the discovery of the feminine and to an acute awareness of his burgeoning manhood. Adolescent dating awakens a girl to the discovery of masculine complementarity as well as of her fast-developing womanhood. Infatuation, transiency and superficiality characterize amorous relationships during this stage of growth. Nonetheless, it is important for self-discovery that we experience such ordinary involvements.

The dating characteristic of young adulthood is a further source of insight into ourselves and consequently into our respective vocations. For the person inclined toward marriage, dating grows more steady and increasingly serious. For a prospective celibate, dating becomes less desirable as a leaning toward more solitary pursuits takes its place. A person interested in remaining single may date different people more or less frequently, but usually without becoming permanently involved with anyone.

(3) *More Significant Choices*

Early in life, people spontaneously develop interests and make choices geared toward a particular lifestyle.

With regard to marriage, for example, a young man weighs carefully the opportunities that a certain career provides in view of support for his future family. A teenage girl, with an eye on eventually caring for a spouse and children, chooses courses in home economics. A young woman enters postgraduate school with contingency plans to integrate her profession with marriage.

With respect to celibacy, for instance, a teenager desiring to encounter Christ more deeply is drawn to seek out short periods of personal prayer or to frequently attend weekday Mass. A young person pursues a profession in which s/he can serve the needy for the sake of Christ.

While making these choices, the person is in fact single. Some of those options pan out. Others do not. Initial interest in one lifestyle increases or wanes. The person may decide to remain single until further indication of a specific direction develops.

In the evolving consciousness of our vocation there comes a time when we know that we are ready for commitment. Some cross that threshold at a clearly identifiable point. Others reach it after a prolonged but observable period of time. Still others realize that they have attained that threshold, yet they are unable to pinpoint the moment or perhaps even the year when it occurred.

CHAPTER 10

Pilgrimage into the Unknown

Our vocation is within us. At the core of becoming fully ourselves is responding faithfully to God's call. Our gift of being is simultaneously a gift of becoming who, how and what the Lord intends us to be.

Since our vocation is within us, discernment of that calling consists in seeking indications of the thrust already integral to our personhood. We have but to look within ourselves to discover the rudiments of our spiritual direction. From the moment of inception, we are in embryonic form who we are meant to be. From that instant too, many people receive a fundamental inclination toward however God intends them to become and toward whatever God desires them to do.

Our calling is thus infinitely more than some vague tendency within us but somehow apart from us. Certainly, our vocation is more than merely the choice of one possibility over several equally viable options. Our spiritual direction actually emerges from within our personhood. The Lord implants within us an innate thrust which, if we freely follow it, enables us to reach optimum union with God and maximum self-development.

So integral to our personhood is God's calling that it produces within us a spiritual imperative. Ultimately, we cannot be, become or do otherwise. In this chapter, we ponder our evolving vocational consciousness from an existential point of view. We say "existential" because our basic calling coincides with our primordial act of existence and extends over the entire course of our life. Hence, consciousness in this context refers to more than cognitive awareness. It bespeaks also a quality of ontological self-identity: We have to eventually encounter our real self and surrender to its imperatives.

A. Horizons of Our Vocation

The gradual emergence of our vocation into consciousness is a veritable pilgrimage into the unknown. At any given point along the way a horizon encircles us. As we advance, our boundaries shift. New horizons appear encompassing new fields of vision. These horizons change according to the specific routes we take, and they evolve according to the forward movement we exert.[1]

Each new horizon presents us with innumerable possibilities. These enhance our openness to God, to the people in our lives and to our own creative powers. From different perspectives a horizon takes on diverse shades and nuances. Amid all the possibilities within our field of vision, we experience an ability to serve God in a variety of ways. Yet, because a horizon also sets limits, it removes at the same time other possibilities. However, we do not usually advert to these limitations at the outset.

The choices that we make in the course of the journey awaken us to a consciousness of our unique vocation. Faced with an array of possibilities, we begin to experience a calling in a certain direction. Desiring to take that option, we let go other alternatives. Thus, our vocation eventually impresses itself upon us as an existential inability to be, become and do otherwise.[2]

The more we choose in accord with our calling, the more limiting our horizons become. This limitedness is not the result of narrow-mindedness, but is the effect of converging upon a goal. God's call thrusts us in the direction of deification. In Christ, "those whom [the Father] foreknows, he also foreordains" (Rom 8:29). That is, God narrows down the possible ways of reaching the goal.

[1]See John Haughey, *Should Anyone Say Forever?* (Garden City, N.Y.: Doubleday, 1975) 42–49; Bernard Lonergan, *Method in Theology* (New York, N.Y.: Herder, 1972) 235–237.

[2]We adapt this expression from a similar one used by Edward Schillebeeckx in *Celibacy* (New York, N.Y.: Sheed & Ward, 1968) 21–25, 120–129.

The pristine Greek meaning of the verb which we translate "foreordain" or "predestine" (*pro-orízo*) is to set limits or to mark off boundaries beforehand. The New Testament meaning of "fore" or "pre" (*pro*) is not the static preprogrammed notion sometimes associated with it, but rather the Hebrew idea of *beterém*. This conjunction gives "before" the sense of "when not yet," as in: "Before forming you in the womb, I knew you" (Jer 1:5). The emphasis of those biblical words is not upon predetermination, but upon God's transcendent freedom and gratuity utterly independent of any merit or action on our part.

Thus, our vocation is not some divinely-inserted microchip or piece of software. It is a sovereignly free gift. It impels us to respond creatively and freely so as to attain optimum freedom and individuality. Our vocation calls us to transcendence in God, even as it becomes enfleshed in our daily life.

(1) *Divergence, Convergence and Emergence*

Usually, the narrowing of our vocational horizons unfolds along the lines of the evolutionary dialectic of divergence, convergence and emergence.

Out of the many possibilities that we see and explore within our immediate field of vision (divergence), we experience that only certain avenues are compatible with God's design for us and with our deepest desires (convergence). Pursuing these avenues, we eventually discover the one to which the Lord is calling us (emergence). That dialectic occurs with regard to to all three dimensions of our vocation: self-identity, lifestyle and mission.

The element of limitation imposed by the horizons of our calling constitutes a positive rather than a negative factor. Our options are gradually narrowed down so that we can choose what God wills. This vocational choice is, furthermore, what we most need in order to advance. God's calling of us to become ourselves in a particular way and the choices we make in accord with the divine will provide the most conducive milieu for interior growth. Without limitations in this positive sense, we would be endlessly flitting from one involvement to another, unable to establish our identity in Christ. We would degenerate into aimless, uncommitted, indecisive drifters.[3]

Not only do horizons shift as routes change, but also our directions vary as our field of vision evolves. Vocation is a dynamic reality, constantly interacting with every aspect of the here and now. Although our calling is gift, we have to work at it moment by moment, for it is not bestowed whole and entire. Each day is new and different:

> The Lord awakens me each morning to listen,
> to listen like a disciple (Isa 50:4).

God invites us daily to relive and to live more fully the calling implanted within us.

(2) *Some Consequences of Evolving Horizons*

The fact that our vocational horizons evolve as we journey to the Father has practical implications.

What lies behind us recedes from view. What lies ahead stretches further and further on. New possibilities persistently confront us. We have to make new choices and deepen our fundamental options. We need to constantly reevaluate our previous commitments in the light of an ever changing field of vision. For example, the love of a couple married twenty-five years would ordinarily be more qualitative than when they were newlyweds. The person who entered the religious life at thirty should have a different perspective on his/her vows at sixty.

Vocational horizons can also shift radically—or, at least judging by externals, it may appear that way. We seem to be heading in one direction, then make a ninety-degree turn, or completely reverse directions. This type of change necessarily throws previous commitments into question. We may discover a need to abandon some former choices in light of the new horizon. Change can at times involve regression. Reversal in some cases indicates an attempt to refuse a calling. However, a new direction can also be the effect of an authentic interior conversion or of a radical new awakening.[4]

[3]See *Spiritual Journey,* 62–74.
[4]See Ibid. 143.

Remaining "committed" solely for commitment's sake can prove both contrary to God's will and profoundly detrimental to personal development.

B. God's Fidelity to God's Calling

The development of God's calling within some people is clearly discernible. For example, at the age of forty a woman sees that the Lord has called her to attain a certain degree of self-identity by living a single life and by teaching for the past twenty years. Moreover, every indication points to the fact that God wants her to continue in that direction.

However, the manner in which God actualizes vocation in many persons is not always so apparent. We cannot reduce the Lord's ways to human categories or expectations (Isa 55:8-9). God does not necessarily follow straight lines or clear-cut patterns. The manner in which God brings a vocation to completion in some individuals transcends all categorization, institutionalization and logic. Sometimes the Lord seems to defy them entirely. A man who made a celibate commitment may discover years later that God is calling him to marriage. A wife may eventually realize that her true calling is to the single life. Change of career is commonplace, especially during midlife.

Moreover, continuous, unconditional acceptance of a calling is not commonplace. Our spiritual genesis incorporates fidelity and infidelity, selflessness and egocentrism, maturity and immaturity, surrender and resistance. While in our deepest selves we desire to remain lovingly receptive, we often find the very opposite in our behavior.

> In fact, this seems to be the rule:
> Every single time I want to do good,
>   something evil comes to hand (Rom 7:21).

There are even occasions when we pursue for a long time directions completely alien to our vocation.

The Lord's loving fidelity endures in and through all this ambivalence:

> If we are unfaithful, Christ Jesus remains ever faithful,
>   for he cannot deny his own self (2 Tim 2:13).

> God's gifts and calling
>   are irrevocable (Rom 11:29).

The Lord persists in seeking us out in love. God irresistibly draws us until we desire only to surrender ourselves freely and joyfully to the Lord.

(1) *An Example from the Experience of Jeremiah*

The prophet's confessions in chapter 20 of the Book of Jeremiah describe in living color his personal experience of the efficaciousness of God's fidelity. Jeremiah begins:

> You burst me wide open, Yahweh (v. 7a).

The verb in question is *pathâh*. Its first meaning is to open wide or enlarge and, in a derived sense, to be persuaded or enticed. In its intensive or piel form—which is what we find in the Hebrew text—the verb suggests a vehement opening up that some translators render "duped," "deceived," "seduced." Jeremiah thus attests that it was none other than the Lord who acted upon him from within him. God split open the depths of the prophet's being to the divine call within, as if Jeremiah's defense mechanisms were so entrenched that only direct vigorous action could pierce or dislodge them. Moreover, the prophet underscores the effectiveness of that divine intervention:

> And I was left utterly exposed (v. 7b).

Jeremiah goes on to affirm that his ability to be receptive to God was itself divine gift:

> You strengthened me, Lord;
>   you enabled me (v. 7c-d).

Many translators render those two verbs "overpower" and "prevail." However, a more literal reading of the text suggests empowering rather than overpowering, enabling rather than prevailing. Thus, Yahweh makes Jeremiah capable of surrendering himself to the Lord's initiative. God, opening up the prophet, does not leave him just gaping, but goes on to render him capable of receiving his vocation.

For Jeremiah, God's calling—especially in terms of mission,

but also lifestyle—meant going counter to virtually all his natural inclinations. Everything in him revolted against his vocation. He labored under serious handicaps: a repulsive appearance, uncontrollable stuttering, an aversion for crowds, a horror of confrontation, etc. His personality manifested traits akin to severe emotional disorder. The prophet's compatriots scorned and ridiculed his option for celibacy. They reviled his preaching of the word. He had to howl violence and ruin every time he spoke. Jeremiah epitomized the experience of his ministry thus:

> The word of Yahweh has meant for me
> insult and derision all day long (v. 8).

In the midst of this upheaval, the prophet decided at one point to quit. He made up his mind to close himself off from God, to try to cut the Lord out of his life:

> I said, "I will not think of Yahweh any longer;
> I will refuse to speak in the Lord's name ever again"
> (v. 9a-b).

Nonetheless, at the very moment he tried to reject God, Jeremiah experienced within his deepest self something impossible to disown:

> There was a fire burning in my heart,
> imprisoned in my bones.
> I fought in vain against it,
> but I could not contain it (v. 9c-f).

This flame rising up within him was his existential inability to be, become and do other than what God's calling demanded. In this inescapable and overwhelming experience of vocation, Jeremiah still tried to kick against the goad. Ultimately, however, he found God's persistent calling impossible to refuse. He experienced himself too weak and too poor to successfully thwart the Lord's work. In the end, the prophet could only willingly let God's call be accomplished in him. The effort to keep fighting the Lord wore him down and wore him out.

The key paradox in the story is this: If Jeremiah had succeeded in denying his vocation, that act would have constituted true violence. That success would have destroyed him. Because

God had enabled him to become receptive and open, the Lord had by the same token disabled Jeremiah from making a definitive refusal of his vocation. God persistently sought him out until he freely desired to accept Yahweh's faithful love.

(2) *An Application to Our Vocational Experience*

As with Jeremiah, so too God persistently draws us until we freely yearn to receive God's faithful love. No matter how intense our resistance, we inevitably reach a threshold where we find the Lord's insistent calling impossible to refuse. In tension-filled hope and in dark faith we desire only to abandon ourselves to God's tender merciful love. Thus, Yahweh's word is effective within us:

> The word which goes forth from my mouth
>   does not return to me empty.
> Rather, it accomplishes what I will
>   and achieves the purpose for which I sent it (Isa 55:11).

CHAPTER 11

Developmental Patterns

In Chapter 9, we presented vocational consciousness as it unfolds through our consistent desires and through ordinary occurrences in our lives. In Chapter 10, we examined vocational development and vocational awareness in relation to evolving horizons and the possibility of permanent commitment. In the present chapter, we consider the mystery of calling from the perspective of developmental patterns leading up to the experience of vocation as an existential inability to be, become or do otherwise.

God's calling is existential because it attains the core of our being. Although the Lord's calling sets in motion the basic thrust of our spiritual direction, our vocation is not fully formed from the outset. As we evolve, so too does God's calling of us. We grow *in* our vocation, *into* it and *because of* it.

Ultimately, our calling is toward the transcendent, toward fullness of life in God. Our calling is a torrent welling up from within us but not of us. It is a force shaping our self-identity, lifestyle and mission on preconscious, prereflective and existential levels. Our vocation is an élan which happens in us rather than a direction which we initiate. We feel our way into our calling rather than deliberately decide upon it in advance. Yet, our acceptance of our evolving vocation and our collaboration with it remain essential to God's plan.

While the thrust of a vocation is bestowed at inception, we recognize only later in life the particulars of that calling. As our vocation evolves, so too does our awareness of it.

The fact that vocational consciousness develops gives rise to certain questions: In order to make a permanent commitment of oneself to God or to another person, how much interior freedom, self-knowledge and vocational awareness are necessary? What are the characteristics typical of vocational consciousness when a person, in response to a sense of having been called by God, is ready to make a lifelong commitment through a Christian lifestyle? How might we identify the developmental patterns of vocational awareness through which a person would ordinarily pass in attaining the freedom, the self-knowledge and the consciousness necessary for permanent commitment?

We distinguish three successive phases of vocational consciousness leading to readiness for lifelong commitment:

- *initial* vocational awareness, characterized by conformity to the established Christian order;
- *advancing* vocational awareness, constituted by the focus on personal relationships with God and with significant others;
- *mature* vocational awareness, consisting in an existential inability to be, become and do otherwise.

That sequence occurs usually in persons raised from childhood in a Christian environment. Theoretically, one can propose optimal parallels between chronological age and those phases of vocational awareness. In actual life, however, chronological age and those phases are only loosely associated. For a variety of reasons, a person can become stuck for years in phase one or two. Pastorally, it is not uncommon to meet a forty-year old individual whose vocational awareness approximates that of an adolescent. On the other hand, we find young people who possess well-developed vocational consciousness. When adults become practicing Christians, their level of vocational consciousness may already be in the advancing or the mature phase.

Our focus in this chapter is the basic characteristics of vocational consciousness as it unfolds *optimally* in each of the above developmental phases. In actual discernment, spiritual guides will have to apply this description in the light of each directee's salvation history. The vocational consciousness necessary for lifelong commitment is unlikely to emerge exactly as we describe it. Nonetheless, something of these developmental patterns is ordinarily observable.

After our discussion of each phase of vocational awareness, we offer insights from three renowned authors. Thus, we present optimal parallels from the research of Brian Hall, James Fowler and Erik Erikson in the field of developmental psychology.[1]

Hall describes four successive phases of consciousness development which usually span the course of a human life: (I) the world as mystery, with self as center; (II) the world as problem to be solved, with self as belonging; (III) the world as project and invention, with self as independent; (IV) the world as mystery cared for, with self as interdependent. Thus, consciousness—that is, the manner in which we perceive the world—advances as we mature.

Fowler examines differences in ways of being which he calls "faithing." He describes the structuring of faith through six successive stages of development: (1) intuitive-projective faith, (2) mythic-literal faith, (3) synthetic-conventional faith, (4) individuative-reflective faith, (5) conjunctive faith and (6) universalizing faith.

According to Erikson, the building and integrating of personality involve an eight-tiered interdependent sequence: trust vs. mistrust; autonomy vs. shame/doubt; initiative vs. guilt; industry vs. inferiority; identity vs. role confusion; intimacy vs. isolation; generativity vs. stagnation; integrity vs. despair. That sequence is based on this principle: Anything that grows has a ground plan out of which the parts arise, each having its time of special ascendancy, until all the parts have arisen to form a functioning whole. Erikson's research indicates that each tier includes a psychosocial crisis which the maturing person has to

---

[1]See *Spiritual Journey,* 228–233; Brian Hall, *The Development of Consciousness: A Confluent Theory of Values* (New York, N.Y.: Paulist, 1976) 49–95. James Fowler, *Stages of Faith: The Psychology of Human Development and the Quest for Meaning* (New York, N.Y.: Harper & Row, 1981) 135–173; *Becoming Adult, Becoming Christian: Adult Development and Christian Faith* (New York, N.Y.: Harper & Row, 1984) 55–64. Erik Erikson, *The Life Cycle Completed* (New York, N.Y.: Norton, 1982) 55–82. Eugene Wright, *Erikson: Identity and Religion* (New York, N.Y.: Seabury, 1982) 51–95.

resolve. Out of the successful resolution of each crisis flows a basic strength or virtue.

A. Initial Vocational Awareness: Conformity to the Established Christian Order

Vocation viewed as fitting into the existing Christian order is the most primitive level of vocational awareness. This level is typically found in children. However, many adults have not advanced appreciably beyond this degree of consciousness.

Who am I? How is the Lord calling me to become myself? What is God calling me to be and to do? Children, in this first stage of vocational awareness, do not ordinarily put these reflective questions to themselves. Should someone else pose them, children are unlikely to give a direct answer. Adults in this phase generally respond with stories about significant events, persons or situations which say something to them about their calling.

In this initial phase, we tend to understand vocation in terms of finding our niche within the established order of the Church or society and of functioning well therein. Moreover, we view that niche in a rather static way, as if God had preset our "place." The thought of not finding our special role can be terrifying, since—as we surmise—it could cause us to miss the mark in this life and perhaps also in the next.

Fidelity to vocation in this phase of consciousness means primarily observing commandments, rules, regulations and traditions. Faithfulness is judged more by the letter of the law than by its spirit.

The God who calls is usually viewed very anthropomorphically. Typically, we see the Lord as judge or as someone up-in-the-sky whose work is to reward the good and to punish the wicked. We imagine heaven, hell, purgatory in a literal, temporal and spatial manner.

Many of us in this initial phase of vocational awareness project aspects of our relationship with our parents onto our rapport with God. We image our Father/Mother in heaven as we experience dad and mom acting toward us: scolding or protecting; too busy to listen or available for nurturing; fighting among themselves or expressing tenderness; yelling and screaming or always being there when we need them; etc. In this phase, whether we view the Lord as benevolent or harsh, we see God as being bound by standards of absolute right and wrong.

Although this incipient vocational consciousness is primitive, it remains a normal developmental phase. It is God who awakens in us an initial awareness of calling. It is the Lord who with tender care guides us as we search for the tasks, roles and ways of being which will furnish us with a sense of belonging to and competency within the Christian community.

Corresponding to this first phase of vocational awareness are Brian Hall's description of consciousness of the world as a problem to be solved, James Fowler's mythic-literal faith and Erik Erikson's psychosocial crisis of industry vs. inferiority.

(1) *Hall: Phase II Consciousness*

Optimally, what Hall designates in his schema as Phase II in the development of consciousness spans the ages of six to sixteen. During those years, most of us view the world as a problem to be solved. Our attention shifts away from self-preservation to the broader issue of coping with and controlling our environment. We expend much energy in the effort to succeed and to belong. Self-esteem and a sense of personal worth arise from becoming useful participants in the existing order.

Children and young adolescents in this phase perceive others—especially parents and teachers—as having control over their world. Adults who have not yet emerged from this phase see clergy, police, managers, etc. as those in control. Having the approval of those authorities is crucial to feeling successful.

(2) *Fowler: Stage 2: Mythic-Literal Faith*

The transition to what Fowler terms mythic-literal faith occurs optimally around the age of six or seven. Some people, however, maintain this faith stance throughout a significant portion of their adult lives.

At this stage, we are capable of concrete operational thinking. We can engage in both inductive and deductive reasoning. Since we can employ rather stable categories of space, time and causality, our assimilation of experience depends less on feeling and fantasy than in the earlier intuitive-projective stage. We thus perceive the world in an orderly, linear and predictable fashion.

In this mythic-literal faith stance, we differentiate our own viewpoints from those of others. This differentiation affords us the capacity for story appreciation. The content of our faith, therefore, relies on the mythic representations of our communities and families. We understand these stories in a literal and concrete manner. Moreover, familiarity with these stories and their values serves as a basis for identification with certain groups and for evaluation of ourselves and others. In this context, we view ourselves and others more in terms of affiliations and actions than in terms of personality, feelings or reflections.

In the stage of mythic-literal faith, we approach moral judgment from the perspective of fairness based on reciprocity. Good is to be rewarded and evil punished.

(3) *Erikson: Industry versus Inferiority*

The psychosocial crisis which Erikson identifies as industry vs. inferiority occurs optimally during the years which precede adolescence. We perceive as significant others most persons with whom we have relationships—parents, siblings, neighbors, teachers, etc. Our primary developmental objective at this time is the mastery of skills and tasks which family and society value. Competency with tools and comfortableness in interaction with the adult world are the emerging virtues of this stage.

B. Advancing Vocational Awareness: Focusing on Personal Relationahips with God and Significant Others

Once we attain a sense of belonging and an ability to function competently within the established Christian order, the question of vocation reemerges. Our vocational consciousness begins to express itself along these lines: I know now that I have a place in the Church and in society. There are roles which I can comfortably fulfill. I can address many of my needs. Yet, who am I really? How am I to become the person the Lord is calling me to be? What can I contribute to God and to the world?

To search out these questions at this phase, we turn to interpersonal relationships. This shift results from the movement of the Spirit abiding in us.

The accent in this advancing vocational consciousness falls first on a personal rapport with God. We no longer experience the Lord primarily as judge, master, almighty, but as friend. Generally, the person of Jesus stands out as we become aware of a thirsting for a more intimate relationship with God. We begin desiring also to contribute creatively to the development of ourselves and of our world for Christ.

The accent in this advancing vocational consciousness falls as well on significant others. Human relationships form the context in which our self-identity and sense of vocation emerge more strongly. We take special notice of how others see us. These perceptions affect us positively or negatively, depending on how we use them. Meaningful vibes strengthen our emerging selfhood and invite heightened vocational awareness. However, there is always the danger of investing significant others with too much power. In that case, we err by trying to conform our choices to their expectations.

A major task of this phase is to test the perceptions that others have of us. Many of these perceptions conflict among themselves. For instance, our parents have one view of us, our peers another. We test those impressions against our experience of ourselves. We try different hats in order to see what fits and what does not.

Although a stronger self-identity is emerging, it is to a large extent a vision of ourselves picked up from others. Our value system, as personally owned, remains virtually unexplored.

As we move through this advancing phase of vocational consciousness, our capacity for reflection increases. We begin to identify threads or patterns running through our salvation history which indicate more of God's will for us.

In relating intimately to Jesus and to significant others, we quicken our capacity to listen to ourselves and to God within us. Through friendship with Jesus and involvements with others, the Spirit opens us more and more to our own mysterious depths where:

I live now, no longer I,

but Christ lives in me (Gal 2:20).

Thus, instead of defining call in terms of our place in the established order, we grope during this advancing vocational awareness toward the experience of vocation as integral to our personhood and as emanating from within us, without being of us.

With respect to our previous study of the critical thresholds and stages of adult spiritual genesis—*The Spiritual Journey*—this second phase of vocational consciousness ordinarily occurs during "Immersion in Creation for Christ."[2] This marks the beginning of what we term "spiritual adulthood."

Brian Hall's Phase II of the development of consciousness, James Fowler's synthetic-conventional faith and Erik Erikson's psychosocial crisis of identity vs. role confusion optimally parallel this second phase of vocational awareness.

(1) *Hall: Phase II Consciousness*

What Hall terms Phase II in his construct of awareness development spans what we call "initial" and "advancing" vocational consciousness.

Certain aspects of Hall's Phase II parallel our description of vocational awareness as conformity to the established order. For instance: As Phase II progresses, we learn to feel increasingly at home in society. Through education, we experience ourselves as professionally competent. Through a sense of belonging, we learn to value ourselves and others.

Other aspects, however, parallel vocational awareness as it is redefined in the light of personal relationships. In Phase II consciousness, our world becomes enlarged beyond narcissistic needs to include the social dimensions of life. We see the universe as existing for everyone. We become aware of the world view of other people. We begin to identify the perspectives of certain institutions on global issues. We seek to gain self-esteem by living up to the expectations of family, peers and established traditions.

[2]See *Spiritual Journey*, 55–59.

(2) *Fowler: Stage 3: Synthetic-Conventional Faith*

This stage is characteristic of adolescence, although many persons persist in it most of their adult lives. The term "synthetic" refers to our ability to form a synthesis of what we know and value. It denotes also that capacity for reasoning whereby we pass from general principles to practical applications. We can now develop a story of our stories by reflecting on our experiences and seeing the patterns which emerge. Personal identity and the meaning of life become burning issues.

Our synthesis is, however, "conventional" because we assume the values and beliefs of a significant group or community. True, we express these in a relatively personal way, but without fully interiorizing them. Typically, our value system as personally owned has not yet become the object of in-depth reflection and critical evaluation. Thus, our sense of authority is still primarily exterior, invested in significant others.

Interpersonal perspective-taking is the key characteristic of this stage. Fowler sums it up this way: "I see you seeing me. I see the me I think you see . . . You see you according to me. You see the you you think I see."[3] Relationships with significant others is now an ever more crucial means of establishing self-identity. Needless to say, discrepancies often exist among the images of ourselves which these significant others mirror to us.

(3) *Erikson: Identity versus Identity Confusion*

The psychosocial crisis of identity vs. diffusion is normal during adolescence. Peer groups attain equal significance with family. Frequently, the barrage of conflicting images and expectations held by these two sources causes us intense confusion and anxiety. As adolescents, we face the challenge of synthesizing our experiences so that we can formulate our own stable sense of identity. Informed self-knowledge and guided reality-testing are important tools for this task.

Qualities such as trust, autonomy and independence—the fruits of successful resolution of previous psychosocial crises—facilitate identity formation. Absence of these qualities leads to increased identity confusion. Fidelity, especially in the sense of

[3]Fowler, *Stages of Faith*, 153.

maintaining commitments in the face of differing value systems, is the basic strength which emerges in the resolution of this crisis.

C. Mature Vocational Awareness: An Existential Inability to Be, to Become and to Do Otherwise

Throughout the stage of spiritual genesis which we designate in an earlier work as "Immersion in Creation for Christ,"[4] our attitude toward the Lord changes as our relationship with God develops. When we were concerned with conformity to the established order, our perceptions of God were primarily as Creator, Almighty, Judge. We respected and feared the Lord. Then, as personal relationships became a catalyst for advancing vocational awareness, we began approaching God as friend.

The Lord uses that newfound intimacy, together with our involvement in creation, to draw us more acutely into mystery. The Spirit leads us to look deeply within ourselves in order to further discern our vocation. As we sift out the images which others have of us and examine the possibilities available to us for lifestyle and mission, we experience a growing need to listen attentively to our deepest selves and to God dwelling within our innermost being.

Plumbing those depths wherein Father, Son and Spirit abide, we come to a peaceful, though not necessarily definable, sense of who we are. There arises the unmistakable intuition of the vocation which is integral to our personhood and which emanates from those mysterious depths. We perceive the general direction of the three interrelated aspects of our calling: self-identity, lifestyle and mission. Our knowledge, consciousness and freedom at this point enable us to perceive our calling in terms of an existential inability to be, to become and to do otherwise. Our spiritual direction asserts itself from within us in the form of a triple imperative:

- I have to be who the Lord calls me to be;
- I must develop in accordance with how God calls me to become;

[4]See *Spiritual Journey*, 59–61.

• I need to do what the Lord sends me forth to accomplish.

Thus, we refer to the third phase of vocational awareness as "mature" consciousness. This phase marks the point at which we perceive the convergence of what God wills for us and of what we most truly desire for ourselves. The depth of this vocational consciousness enables us to embark upon lifelong commitments in response to the Lord's calling. However, while our vocational awareness is mature in relation to the two previous phases, that maturity is far from perfect. Completion of our calling, vocational consciousness and commitment requires the rest of our life. Chapter 15 of this book outlines that further development.

Although the phrase "existential inability . . ." is couched in negative terms, it expresses a dynamically positive reality.

In itself, the word "inability" can refer to the fact that many people experience their vocation somewhat negatively. For example: I do not feel called to marriage or celibacy; therefore, I'll remain single. I am not inclined to military service or the Peace Corps, so I'll stay in college. That attitude, however, would be more characteristic of initial vocational consciousness than of the mature phase which we are describing.

In this context, "inability" accentuates the intensity and urgency of our need to respond voluntarily to God in the manner that God wills. Thus, when we say "inability to be otherwise," we affirm primarily an ontological imperative. In the realm of being, we come to be our transformed selves by becoming in the way God desires. Becoming ourselves in the specific way appropriate for us then gives rise to a moral imperative—an inability to become and to do otherwise. Our lifestyle and our behavior flow from our personhood.

Brian Hall's Phase III development of consciousness, James Fowler's individuative-reflective faith and Eric Erikson's psychosocial crisis of intimacy vs. isolation offer optimal parallels with vocational consciousness experienced as an existential inability to be, to become and to do otherwise.

(1) *Hall: Phase III Consciousness*

This phase ordinarily spans the ages of sixteen to midlife. In it, we are no longer dependent on the world as defined by significant others. Living up to their expectations is less important than being ourselves. Self-affirmation lessens the need for approval from others. Our primary needs are self-directedness and independence. A sense of personal power and inner authority replaces institutional control and the desire for conformity.

We now view the world as a project to be improved. We long to act upon it and to reshape it. Thus, creativity, imagination and responsible stewardship become primary values around which we organize our life. Social justice, liberation and freedom for self and others become priorities.

(2) *Fowler: Stage 4: Individuative-Reflective Faith*

Fowler observes that two movements converge in the transition from synthetic-conventional faith to individuative-reflective faith.

First, a shift in the sense of grounding and orientation of the self occurs. We begin to act from our inner authority rather than from a self-concept based on interactions with significant others. An "executive ego" emerges. We can differentiate our real self from the roles and relationships in which we engage.

Second, we take a reflective stance toward our value system. What was previously tacit and unexamined becomes the object of critical reflection. What is personally meaningful is separated from what is not. We make an explicit choice of our beliefs, values and commitments. They are integrated into a consciously ratified and personally owned value system.

(3) *Erikson: Intimacy versus Isolation*

This psychosocial crisis arises optimally during early adulthood. Once basic self-identity has been established, the challenge then consists in sharing ourselves in communion with other significant persons. Self-disclosure and willingness to remain vulnerable facilitate this intimacy. Altruistic love is the basic virtue which emerges in the resolution of this crisis.

D. Summary

Throughout our spiritual genesis the Lord directs us in our deepening consciousness of God's personal calling for us. In so doing, the Lord ordinarily interacts and cooperates with the natural processes of human growth and development. These processes are physical, cognitive, emotional, social, sexual, psychological and spiritual.

At first, in our efforts to discern our vocation we look outside ourselves for a direction. We do this because we perceive God to be outside us. Yet, the Lord uses those efforts and perceptions as a foundation for the development of an initial vocational awareness. At some point, however, we undergo a change of focus. Through involvement with creation, especially with persons, God brings us to realize that our calling is within us and that only certain choices can actualize our vocation.

In this chapter, we described a threefold developmental sequence through which God ordinarily brings a person to sufficient vocational consciousness for lifelong commitment. The following schema summarizes: (1) those three phases, (2) their place in relation to certain critical thresholds and stages in our book *The Spiritual Journey,* and (3) their optimal parallels with three researchers in the field of developmental psychology: Hall, Fowler and Erikson.

Vocation. Consc.	Spiritual Journey	Brian Hall	James Fowler	Erik Erikson
Initial Vocation. Awareness	Tending toward Immersion	Phase II Development of Con-sciousness	Stage 2: Mythic-Literal Faith	Industry versus Inferiority
Advancing Vocation. Awareness	Threshold and Stage of Immersion in Creation for Christ		Stage 3: Synthetic-Convent. Faith	Identity versus Identity Confusion
Mature Vocation. Awareness		Phase III Develop. of Consc.	Stage 4: Individu.-Reflect. Faith	Intimacy versus Isolation

LIFELONG
COMMITMENT
TO GOD'S
DEVELOPING CALL

CHAPTER 12

Vocational Commitment

In creating us, God implants within the depths of our person-hood the thrust of a vocation. From inception, we begin becoming who the Lord calls us to be. From the womb already, we start inching toward how God wills us to become our true selves. From the outset too, we commence groping toward what the Lord destines us to do. Throughout life's journey our self-identity, lifestyle and mission develop and interact along the lines of the Lord's calling.

Of the three elements which constitute vocation, the most fundamental is self-identity—who God wills us to be. Ultimately, that consists in being our unique selves transformed in God. Whatever our weakness or resistance, the Lord makes everything work somehow toward our personal deification (Rom 8:28).

The fact that self-identity remains the most basic dimension of vocation does not detract from the importance of vocational lifestyle and mission. All three are equally from God and to God. Moreover, as these components of God's calling unfold, our consciousness of each one also evolves. That emerging voca-tional awareness thrusts us in the direction of commitment.

In this chapter we consider more explicitly our response to the Lord's calling—that is, our commitment. We examine how commitment forms and how it becomes lifelong. We explore commitment primarily in relation to vocational lifestyle.

115

A. The Meaning of Commitment

The noun "commitment" comes from a Latin verb denoting to consign or to entrust. As a verb, it can refer to handing someone over to the charge or trust of another, for example, the courts committing a person to a correctional or mental institution. Commitment in everyday parlance means an agreement or a promise to do something in the future.

Commitment in the context of Christian vocation, however, transcends those meanings. It evokes a loving steadfastness which flows from the exigencies of an interpersonal relationship. Commitment is the effect of a covenant. And permanent commitment is the outcome of a lasting covenant.

It is not enough that we commit ourselves to some-thing—to a way, an institution or a task. Nothing less than the personal can satisfy our deepest yearnings. Moreover, what most radically characterizes personhood is our infinite capacity to love and to be loved. Vocational commitment has to be therefore inherently interpersonal and based on mutual entrusted love.

Experience teaches that not even commitment to another person or several persons brings ultimate fulfillment. In fact, involvement in intimate relationships only whets our appetite for more and more of "an-I-don't-know-what."[1] While these created relationships remain very meaningful, they providentially point us beyond themselves. Thus, they open our hearts to their source — to God who is Love (1 John 4:16).[2]

Commitment then, in a vocational context, ultimately means surrender of ourselves in faith, hope and love to Father, Son and Spirit who have first entrusted themselves to us (1 John 4:10). Commitment is a "giving of [our] deepest to [God] whose depth has no end."[3] It is an opening and an offering of what is most mysterious and loving in us to that which is most mysterious and loving in Father, Son and Spirit. Vocational commitment postulates not only covenant, but also communion and partnership in love with the Trinity.

[1] St. John of the Cross, poem: *The Spiritual Canticle*, stanza 7.
[2] See *O Blessed Night*, 57–68; *Receptivity*, 17–31.
[3] Pierre Teilhard de Chardin, *The Divine Milieu* (New York, N.Y.: Harper Torchbooks, 1957) 128.

Commitment between God and an individual is the bond or covenant in which human response to the Lord's calling occurs. In a sense, evolving self-identity, lifestyle and mission are the fruits of the loving, ever intensifying self-giving of God and a person to each other.

B. Choice of Vocational Lifestyle

When we say: "I decide to marry; I choose celibacy; I resolve to remain single," we need to realize that those statements presuppose a divine initiative of long duration. The process begins with God in us implanting the movement toward a vocational lifestyle. It continues with God nurturing the process along. It reaches maturity with God bringing our vocation explicitly into consciousness.

Therefore, when we say "I decide . . ." or "I choose . . ." or "I resolve . . ." it is because that decision, choice or resolution has already been made in us. Who made it then, God or me? Actually, both God and me. Basic vocational decisions are made by God and the person working together. The Lord initiates, nurtures and matures the choices which become commitments. Yet, we make them too, first preconsciously, then semi-reflectively and finally deliberately. Throughout this entire process we are cooperating with God and God is collaborating with us.

A vocation to a Christian lifestyle attains the very core of our being. It is an ontological reality in us even before it is known by us or becomes the object of reflection. Thus, we think, choose and live the way we do because of who we are. Our self-identity spontaneously interacts with how God calls us to become ourselves in Christ, because our calling to a basic vocational lifestyle is so integral to who we are.

As our calling matures and our awareness of it develops, what was preconscious and then semi-reflective in our response to God becomes volitional. What began in us, but without us, is now in us with our assent, consent and cooperation. What God formed in secret is now coming to light. Thus, we say "yes" to what is and to what has been. We commit ourselves. The living out of that commitment in turn exerts an increasingly formative influence on every facet of our being, becoming and doing.

C. Permanency of Commitment

In order for us to make a permanent vocational commitment, two conditions must converge: the consciousness of interpersonal intimacy with God and the experience of a particular calling as an inability to be, become or do otherwise. Ordinarily, those two prerequisites for permanence in commitment become discernible in the phase of mature vocational consciousness. Their existence presupposes that we have established a basic self-identity in Christ and thereby reached spiritual adulthood.

(1) *Commitment and Evolving Vocational Consciousness*

Commitment, as a covenant of love with God, requires considerable personal maturity. We have to pass through a lengthy process of holistic growth before we are capable of this self-giving. Our capacity for commitment, together with the quality of commitment itself, develops throughout the three phases of vocational consciousness.

In initial vocational awareness, we view our calling in terms of conformity to the established order. We measure self-worth according to our skill in exercising various roles offered to us in the Church and society. Our capacity for committing ourselves at this time is thus directed primarily to things rather than to the personal. While this situation is a providential phase of emerging vocational consciousness, it remains a transitional one. For as soon as we succeed in committing ourselves to this conformity, we find that it can no longer sustain us. To persevere, we need more.

In advancing vocational awareness, we forge ahead in the direction of the personal. Our relationships with God and with significant others become a primary value. Even though we are growing in self-knowledge, the expectations of others exert considerable influence on our self-concept. Vocational consciousness and the capacity for commitment are definitely on the increase. We may find ourselves even strongly inclined toward a specific lifestyle.

Nonetheless, permanent commitment at this time would be premature. Until we can establish sufficient self-identity to recognize unmistakably our existential inability to become otherwise, we cannot adequately discern to what degree our choices flow from a sense of vocation and to what extent they result from the influence of significant others. In advancing vocational awareness, we grow in the conviction that our lifestyle and ministry must be expressive of who we are, yet the impact of a mature spiritual imperative is not sufficiently present to validate lifelong commitment.

It is in the phase of maturing vocational consciousness that most people experience God's calling as a existential inability to be, become or do otherwise. That spiritual imperative flowing from vibrant loving communion with the indwelling Trinity constitutes the basis for permanency in vocational commitment. There are many principles for discerning a possible calling to a Christian lifestyle. However, the experience of a particular lifestyle as an existential inability remains the definitive sign of vocational authenticity.

(2) *Commitment and Self-identity*

Maturity in self-knowledge, growth in freedom and awareness of the world around us go hand in hand with the consciousness of our vocation as an existential inability.

Why do those qualities have to coincide before we are ready for permanent commitment? The crux of the response is self-identity.

Self-identity and personhood refer to the same reality, but from different points of view. Personhood accentuates ontologically who we are—"I am me." Self-identity suggests consciousness of who we are—"I know I am me." Both personhood and self-identity are present in embryonic form from our initial act of existence. Throughout life, we work with God as God forms, evolves and matures them. At some point in this process of self-development, self-knowledge and self-love, we attain an explicit sense of who we are. We reach mature self-identity.

Sufficient self-identity is a prerequisite for authentic vocational commitment. Why? If we hope to surrender our-selves to God, we must first have a "self" to give. We cannot entrust to the Lord a self that is not yet adequately formed and known.

Vocational development, consciousness development and self-development occur simultaneously. The ensuing sense of selfhood enables us to discern which directions are compatible with who we really are. It enables us to perceive the lifestyles to which God calls us. It enables us to choose the ministries to which the Lord sends us. In a word, self-identity renders us capable of voluntarily committing ourselves to God through a vocational lifestyle and mission.

God dwelling within us guides us always toward what is compatible with the gift of our inmost self. God's calling evokes our commitment in response. We interact and collaborate with the Lord throughout the process of our vocational maturation. Yet, until we experience the vocation residing in us as an existential inability, we cannot know which calling will ultimately emerge. Until we experience a spiritual imperative regarding a specific vocation, we are not ready for permanency of commitment. That truth entails far-reaching pastoral implications.

CHAPTER 13

Pastoral Implications Related to Lifelong Commitments

From an evolutionary and relational perspective, discernment of vocational lifestyle has as its underpinnings the following principles:

- As our calling develops, so too vocational awareness. As that consciousness evolves, so too our covenant with the Lord and our commitment to the Lord.
- All lifelong vocational commitment is ultimately to God, rather than to an institution or a human person.
- God does not expect us to commit ourselves permanently in a specific Christian lifestyle until we have sufficiently developed a self to give and until God has produced in us ontological, moral and spiritual imperatives to do so.
- We do not have the right to demand of ourselves or others more than the Lord requires.

In the light of those principles, we and our spiritual guides must wait out both the development of our calling and the emergence of mature vocational consciousness. That waiting in faith entails listening and doing, receptivity and activity. That waiting paves the way for permanent commitment and covenanting.

Thus, we continue collaborating with God in the work of developing ourselves and our world until we experience in sufficient depth who we are in Christ. Attainment of that fundamental self-identity then disposes us to perceive with sufficient cogency the vocational direction already forming within us. This perception in turn enables us to recognize the ontological, moral and spiritual imperatives to become fully ourselves through a God-given lifestyle and mission.

By *ontological imperative* we mean that urgency which lies at the core of our being as being, prior to our reflecting upon its presence or acting voluntarily out of its thrust. This imperative is integral to our calling to be and to become all that God destines for us. It exercises its mandate whether or not we avert explicitly to its presence. Nonetheless, this imperative gradually impresses itself upon our consciousness and ekes out our willing cooperation in pursuing its goal.

By *moral imperative* we refer to the influence of that ontological urgency upon our attitudes and behavior, especially as they become increasingly voluntary. The word "moral" denotes conscious relatedness to both God and creation, as our vocational lifestyle and mission bring us into ever more qualitative interaction with God and creatures.

By *spiritual imperative* we understand the impetus toward Spirit and spiritualization which the transformative activity of God within us exercises on our vocation and developing awareness.

Therefore, in order to bind in conscience, a permanent commitment—whether represented by vows or by promises, in public or in private—must be a conscious voluntary statement of an already existing interior reality. Commitment does not cause vocation; rather, it flows from vocation and proclaims it. Permanent commitment celebrates what our ontological, moral and spiritual imperatives affirm has been, is and will continue to be.

A. Premature and Mature Lifelong Commitments

Approaching commitment as a voluntary response to an already existing interior calling, we distinguish "premature" commitment to God in marriage or celibacy from "mature." This contrast is similar to—but not exactly identical with—the distinctions between incomplete and complete, moving toward and having arrived, putative and authentic, binding in the external forum and bonded interiorly.

By mature marital commitment, we mean a monogamous sacramental covenant in its full theological and spiritual sense. We understand mature celibate commitment as a personal consecration which radically changes the course of one's life according to these two logia of Jesus: "for my sake and for the gospel" (Mark 10:29); "for the sake of [God's] reign" (Matt 19:12). Throughout this work we concentrate on the internal forum—the realm of conscience, the realm of God calling a person from within. We prescind from matters and judgments related to the external forum of civil and ecclesial law. These have their importance and relevancy, but unless we explicitly advert to them, we leave to others that aspect of the question.

Everyone is born single. At some point along the way, most people experience a vocation to marry, many choose to remain single and a few are called to celibacy. Passage from singlehood to wedded Christian couple begins when two persons experience that they love each other in such a way that they need to share the remainder of their mortal life in a covenant relationship and express that bondedness sacramentally in marriage. Passage from singlehood to celibacy takes place very privately between a person and the Lord, in God's time and in God's way. This transition does not automatically come about at the end of the novitiate or after a certain number of years in formation.

Mature marital and celibate commitments are those which result from deliberate choice, from having reached an existential inability to become otherwise. These marital and celibate commitments arise out of an interior sense of vocation which is ratified by ontological, moral and spiritual imperatives. Mature marital and celibate commitments can be termed *de facto* commitments. That is, as-a-matter-of-fact the exterior situation accurately expresses the interior reality. Experiencing a call from God to marriage or celibacy, these persons freely seek to become more fully themselves in that lifestyle. Their consecration or vows celebrate what has already occurred and what continues to deepen.

Premature marital and celibate commitments, on the other hand, are those which to all intents and purposes appear authentic from the outside, but in reality lack something essential for permanency. They are not supported by adequate awareness of the ontological, moral and spiritual imperatives necessary for perseverance. For people in such situations, the interior and the exterior, the within and the without of their lives, do not synchronize, or at least have not yet come into basic harmony.

(1) *Premature Commitments*

There are basically two contexts in which people discover that their commitments were premature: (a) Once mature vocational awareness occurs, the committed person sees that s/he made a serious mistake. (b) Once mature vocational consciousness dawns, the committed individual realizes that initially s/he made the correct option, although prematurely.

(a) *A First Scenario: A Mistake Was Made.* Although not really called by God to a particular lifestyle, some persons faced with the option of permanent commitment proceed nonetheless in that direction.

What would prompt someone to make a lifelong commitment when no such vocation exists? There could be many reasons. Here are a few: Insincere individuals might deliberately fake a commitment for monetary gain, power or pleasure. Well-meaning but shallow persons might enter into a commitment for the sake of convenience or security. Poor judgment, inadequate discernment or incompetent guidance leads other people to engage in a direction which their interior thrust cannot sustain.

Some premature marital commitments arise out of arranged marriages. These were commonplace at certain periods of Western history and still prevail in many cultures. Today in the West, arranged marriages occur occasionally among the wealthy and the status-conscious. Other premature marital commitments—widespread among the too young, the naive and the inexperienced—result from virtually no discernment at all or from precipitous closure on the discernment process.

Premature celibate commitments result from approaching celibacy as if it were little more than a required appendage for some ministry or for membership in an institute. Celibacy in that case is the "right thing to do" in order to attain a desirable goal. The wish to live up to the expectations of others or the belief that celibacy is in itself somehow a superior way to holiness motivates some people in making premature celibate commitments.

Many premature commitments are binding *de jure*. According to both civil and ecclesial law, a couple may be living in a legal marriage. However, they realize later that their life together does not correspond to the inner dynamics of their personal vocations. What are they to do? A Roman Catholic priest may have chosen presbyteral ordination and have accepted the celibate obligation which presently accompanies it, without also experiencing a personal calling to celibacy. What does he do, then, if later he discerns a vocation to marriage? When people involved in such situations become conscious of the discrepancy between their interior truth and their exterior lifestyles, some seek divorce, dispensation or declaration of nullity. Others try to live out the contradiction as best they can. Releasing some of these people from juridical bonds poses formidable dilemmas for the legal establishment. Yet, forcing these people to live soul-rending contradictions imposes intolerable burdens on them.

Our experience of helping people discern God's will and make sense out of their disjointed lives impels us to address certain thorny issues which underlie those perplexing questions. In so doing, we hope to contribute to a better understanding of the mystery of vocation and to point toward more satisfying avenues of resolution for those trapped in the quagmire of having to choose between their conscience and the institutional element of the Church.

Theoretically at least, any calling is still possible at the time of a premature marital or celibate commitment. Neither the person nor his/her spiritual guides can presume the final outcome. Interiorly, there has existed a subtle movement in a certain direction—the direction in which God has been calling the discernee all along. The individual's premature marital or celibate commitment would then be the context in which the Lord eventually brings forth mature vocational consciousness. As the person nears that breakthrough, signs become increasingly cogent and the ontological, moral and spiritual imperatives more recognizable. However, until the actual existential inability dawns, closure on the discernment process can have agonizing long-range effects on a person's life.

Whatever force a "vow" may have in the external forum for individuals caught in premature commitments, it cannot be permanently binding in the internal forum. If God has not really called a person to a particular vocational lifestyle, there is no interior basis for a vow. There may be a juridical bond, but no spiritual covenant exists. There may be legally binding obligations which have to be addressed, but those factors do not of themselves constitute a calling. What the Lord has not brought about cannot bind permanently before God.

Premature marital or celibate commitments are not necessarily or even entirely negative situations, even when they are shown to have been mistakes. Many Christians enter into these predicaments with sincerity and goodwill. When they pronounce their vows, they are doing the best they can with the light they have at the time. In their personal lives they continue to mature and make many positive contributions to society and the Church. These people work with the Lord, and God interacts with them every step along the way. However, they have not yet discovered their definitive vocational lifestyle. It could lie in another direction, and indeed sometimes does.

When permanently committed spouses or celibates realize with prayerful discernment and competent guidance that they have made a mistake regarding their basic vocational lifestyle, they frequently seek release from the juridical implications of what they come to consider an interiorly non-binding vow. A viable pastoral procedure would be: first, to be granted a declaration of nullity regarding the interior aspects of the premature commitment, and then, to be granted a dispensation or a divorce in regard to the external forum. What God has not actually initiated or joined together will not last. Nor should we require it to do so.

(b) *A Second Scenario: The Correct Choice Was Made, although Prematurely.* Another context of premature commitment is the following: An interior vocation to the lifestyle in question exists, but the person permanently commits him/herself prior to having attained sufficient vocational awareness. In this case, the premature commitment is in fact tending toward maturity. The commitment is, therefore, both interiorly and exteriorly true, even if it be immature and precipitous.

For some individuals, what happened too early turns out to

be fortuitous. What started off principally *de jure* ends up also *de facto*. The dawning of vocational imperatives could occur in one fell swoop, like waking up suddenly at midday. Or the awakening can be protracted over many months or years. In either case, these people are happy indeed, because they come to realize that they were making the correct decisions all along.

The fact remains, however, that making a premature commitment is still putting the cart before the horse, even if the situation is eventually rectified. At the time the vows were pronounced, the outcome could have, theoretically at least, gone another way. Permanent commitment requires sufficient self-knowledge, consciousness and freedom. Experience of a vocation as an existential inability is a sign sine qua non of a person's capacity and readiness for lifelong commitment.

(2) *Passage from Singlehood to a Permanent Celibate Commitment*

Generally, when people begin thinking even vaguely about vocational lifestyles, they are as a matter of fact single. That means, among other things, that they are unmarried, yet open to and available for marriage. If they are attracted to presbyteral ministry or religious life, these persons cannot but notice that those vocations exclude marriage. Celibacy as a distinct lifestyle chosen out of a sense of personal calling, however, rarely occurs to them at this early phase of vocational awareness.

As a vocation to the presbyterate or the religious life asserts itself, many of these people enter a seminary or a pre-novitiate program. For the moment, they are living celibately. That is, they are unmarried and unavailable for marriage because of the vocational direction which they are in the process of discerning. They are moving toward a possible clerical or religious celibate commitment.

If they persevere in one of those vocational directions, these persons are eventually presented for presbyteral ordination, perpetual vows or both. This is when the crunch regarding vocational consciousness strikes with full force. Juridically, presbyteral ordination (at least for now) and perpetual vows are permanently binding with respect to celibacy. What then is the maturity of the candidate's vocational awareness specifically with regard to celibacy as a permanent calling to an all-embracing and all-penetrating lifestyle?

At this point, people engaged in vocational discernment encounter variations of the following scenarios:

(a) God has brought me to mature vocational consciousness. I now experience a calling to celibacy essentially as an existential inability to become otherwise. Call it what you will, I am in effect unmarriageable[1] for the sake of Christ and the gospel (Mark 10:29), for the sake of the reign of God (Matt 19:12). Experiencing an ontological, moral and spiritual imperative to commit myself permanently to God as a celibate, I will proceed with a formal expression of that reality and move forward in living out that commitment for the rest of my life.

(b) I cannot yet honestly say that I have arrived at the experience of a calling to celibacy as an existential inability to become otherwise. Although I have been living celibately as well as I can, I am not at this time, strictly speaking, unmarriageable for the sake of Christ and the gospel. However, I believe that God is drawing me in that direction. In the hope that my sense of vocational lifestyle is correct, I will proceed with a lifelong celibate commitment. If I discover later that my decision was a mistake, I will then deal with the situation.

(c) Not only have I not yet arrived at the experience of a calling to celibacy as an existential inability to become otherwise, but I experience myself as quite marriageable—even desirous of marriage. I have been living what some might term "minimal celibacy," that is, I am not presently sexually active. Yet, I feel called to presbyteral ordination or seek full affiliation with a religious institution. Therefore, I choose to assume the juridical obligations of a lifelong celibate commitment. I hope that my ministry or liking for this community will sustain indefinitely my sexual abstinence.

(d) Not being able to apply the rudiments of mature vocational consciousness to myself, I choose to put off ordination or perpetual vows for the purpose of further discernment. Until I

---

[1]See Edward Schillebeeckx, *Celibacy* (New York, N.Y.: Sheed & Ward, 1968) 21–25, 75–110. Our forthcoming book on discerning vocations to marriage, celibacy and singlehood treats in detail the "unmarriageability" of the celibate called by God.

experience the ontological, moral and spiritual imperatives which accompany mature vocational awareness, I will not make a lifelong commitment.

In this scenario, the candidate's delay must be tested. Only once the indecision is discerned to be primarily from God and not other influences would s/he be encouraged to wait out the postponement. Some people experience extreme difficulty in making up their minds about anything of consequence. Others are incapable of permanent commitment in any form. Still others tend to postpone lifelong decisions until they are "absolutely sure," which for most would mean never. No matter how cogent one's interior imperatives are, lifelong vocational commitment is always a leap in faith.

(3) *Passage from Singlehood to a Permanent Marital Commitment*

When most individuals begin considering marriage, they are in fact single and are looking for an appropriate spouse. Thus, they are inclined toward conjugal life, but do not yet know with whom. Marriage understood specifically as a vocation may or may not have occurred to them.

Persons moving toward lifelong celibate commitments ordinarily live celibately for many years before formal consecration. For better or for worse, prospective spouses are not permitted to test the authenticity of their marital calling in the same way. Moreover, their discernment is compounded by the fact that marriage entails the convergence of two callings. Frequently, the couple are at different stages of vocational consciousness. Too often, one or both have no vocational awareness at all.

People involved in marriage preparation or marriage counseling encounter a variety of situations. We offer a few of the more common scenarios: first in the context of marriage preparation, and then in the context of marriage counseling.

(a) *In the Context of Marriage Preparation.* (1) Both prospective spouses are so in love with each other that they experience the essence of what we have termed "an existential inability" to become other than married. Moreover, they want and need to celebrate that conjugal intimacy in a sacramental manner. Such maturity of vocational consciousness is, however, rare at the time of most weddings.

(2) One of the engaged persons has attained mature vocational awareness, the other has not. Yet, there is hope that s/he will eventually do so. The couple insist on proceeding with the wedding, and trust that their love will sustain them.

(3) Neither prospective spouse has reached mature vocational consciousness. Yet, they press on toward the wedding, willing to make the tough choices if their marriage does not work out.

(4) The couple, although they desire an elaborate church wedding, have no inkling of marriage as a vocation. They have no meaningful sense of being called by God to share a lifelong covenant relationship. They just want to get married and then see what develops.

(5) The prospective spouses are willing to postpone the ecclesial celebration of their marriage until both have experienced mature vocational awareness. In this situation, some decide to live together, others enter into a civil marriage, while still others choose to remain engaged.

(b) *In the Context of Marriage Counseling.* (1) The man and the woman had fallen in love and wanted to marry one another. There was little or no vocational consciousness at the time. Years later, they realize that, regardless of what God's will may have been in the past, the Lord is now calling them to remain married until death parts them.

(2) One spouse has attained mature vocational awareness, only to realize that God is calling him/her to marry somebody other than the one with whom s/he is presently living. What to do, especially when children are involved?

B. Single by Circumstance or by Choice, for a Time or for Life

When we speak of singlehood as a vocational lifestyle, we refer to singlehood positively chosen for the sake of Christ and the gospel. People opt for the single life for many reasons other than an awareness of a calling from the Lord, for example: to care for aging parents, for the sake of a profession, because one really likes living alone. These persons are truly single. Their options may be quite altruistic in many instances. However, a sense of vocation does not automatically accompany their choice of the single life. In terms of vocational awareness, they may be still in a preconscious or initial phase.

With respect to the single life, some persons are single by circumstance—by fate, as it were—and others are single by deliberate choice. One thinks, for example, of a man who is single solely because no one would marry him in contrast to a professional woman who voluntarily wishes to remain single. Some people begin single by circumstance and evolve into singlehood as a freely chosen lifestyle. If single by choice flows from a sense of vocation, it could indeed be indicative of a calling to singlehood.

Single by circumstance covers a myriad of nuances and possibilities. Many spouses and celibates who made premature lifelong commitments are single at heart. Some singles want desperately to marry, but cannot. Others do not want the responsibilities of wedded life, but neither do they desire the solitude of celibacy or the loneliness of singlehood. These persons more or less fall through the cracks of the three basic vocational lifestyles which we describe. Still others happen to be single for the moment because they are on their way to either marriage or celibacy.

Single by choice for many people ultimately means remaining single out of at least a vague sense of vocation. These persons knowingly and willingly choose to develop themselves as single for their own sake and more or less intentionally also for the sake of God and others. The specific awareness of a calling to this lifestyle may be explicit, latent or couched in some personal value or pursuit which for them excludes celibacy and marriage.

Another approach to the single life considers singlehood in terms of negative or positive motivation.

An illustration of singlehood based on negative motivation is people living this lifestyle because it befalls them. Nothing else seems to work. They do not really want to be single, but they stick with it. Some who are single by circumstance are negatively so. On the other hand, many single by circumstance experience their way of life as positive and fulfilling even though they did not specifically choose it. Some who begin with negative motivation change their attitude. They positively accept to remain single, even if given a viable alternative they might opt otherwise.

Another example of the motivational approach is people who make a deliberate choice for singlehood based on negative or positive reasoning. An example of negative reasoning would be choosing to be single because one does not like the other possibilities. Thus, the single option seems less threatening, less difficult, less exigent for the individual. An example of positive reasoning would be a person's option to remain single because s/he experiences singlehood as more fulfilling than any other lifestyle.

Singlehood—whether by circumstance or by choice, whether negative or positive—can be either for a time or for the rest of one's earthly sojourn.

What some people today call the single life may be in effect an informal expression of a veritable celibate lifestyle. For a variety of reasons, they may not care to use the terms "consecration," "celibacy" or even "Christ." Nonetheless, the inner thrust of the reality is, by any other name, celibacy.

The converse may also be true, namely: We find couples of so-called "singles"—homosexual as well as heterosexual—living together in deep bonds of love and mutual commitment. These domestic partnerships may not qualify as juridically or ecclesially acceptable marriages. Yet, the quality of these persons' lives transcends what some might moralistically call "living in sin."

CHAPTER 14

The Responsibility of the Christian Community in Vocational Awakening

In this chapter, we use the expression "Christian community" to include both the family and the local group of believers in Christ Jesus. It is ordinarily from within the Christian community that God causes vocation to emerge. Each member of the community and the group as a whole influence our calling and our response to it.

Ideally, the Christian community is the supportive and challenging context in which we experience our faith and live out our vocation amidst a diversity of charisms:

> To each of us grace has been bestowed
> according to the measure of Christ's gift . . .
> to prepare God's people for the work of service,
> so that they may build up the Body of Christ,
> until we all reach unity in faith
> and in full knowledge of the Son of God.
> Thus, we will become mature
> with the fullness of Christ himself (Eph 4:7, 12-13).

We describe four significant dimensions of the Christian community's role in the vocational formation of its members.[1]

[1]See James Fowler, *Becoming Adult, Becoming Christian* (New York, N.Y.: Harper & Row, 1984) 128–147.

These are: witnessing, education, discernment and emancipation.

A. Witnessing

In the New Testament, the call to witness presupposes personal experience of the mystery to which God commissions an
individual to testify. Witnessing requires also a certain wisdom
and insight obtained from direct encounter with God. Its purpose is to invite and to enable others to participate in mystery.[2]

The biblical notion of witnessing involves both active and
passive elements. On the one hand, to witness is to do something. It means attesting to the truth of someone or something,
even to the point of martyrdom if necessary. To witness is to actualize in our lives evangelical values and convictions and then
to proclaim them by word and example. On the other hand, witnessing is something that the Lord does through us. Jesus proclaims his Good News in and through our being and our action.
Witnessing in this sense requires loving receptivity on our part.
It means letting truth shine through our personhood, attitudes
and behavior. It is being a "light to the world" (Matt 5:14).

God calls the Christian community to witness to vocation as
an evangelical value. Many communities, however, flounder in
the implementation of this responsibility. Part of the problem
lies with adult Christians themselves. Many lack the mature vocational consciousness necessary to effectively foster a sense of
God's calling in young community members. These adults have
little or no idea how to approach this mystery in their own lives,
let alone how to help others discern their calling. Considerable
difficulty in vocational development is related also to situations
within contemporary Western society.

(1) *Situations in Western Society Which Affect Communal
Discernment of Vocations*

The feminist movement has posed a formidable challenge to
patriarchal society. This movement has exposed the injustice of
the commonly accepted male-dominance/female-submission
pattern of interaction. This crisis in relationship leaves no area of

[2]See *TDNT*, IV:474–508.

Western life untouched, including the Church. While a majority of people agree that change is inevitable, debate continues over what should replace the old modes of interrelating. Underlying this issue is an even more basic question—gender identity. What do "masculine" and "feminine" really mean?

Ours is an age of mobility. People living in rural areas move to urban centers to eke out a living. Business firms routinely transfer employees and their families from one city to another, from one nation to another. Modern transportation makes worldwide travel accessible to almost everyone. While this mobility can broaden horizons, it allows fewer people to establish roots. Many persons do not experience the stability and continuity of growing up in the same community. Often, they have little or no contact with their extended families. Consequently, mobility affects the transmission of cultural values and ecclesial traditions.

The level of material progress in Western societies has also provoked something of a crisis. With the availability of goods, money and pleasurable pursuits at their fingertips, many Christians grapple with how to use these resources in a manner consistent with the gospel. Rapid technological advancement raises issues of ethics and value in every branch of science. Some people would simply condemn all technology as evil. Others practically worship it. Most of us, without espousing either extreme, perceive these discoveries and inventions as basically positive, yet all too easily seductive. We search for ethical and moral norms that will enable humankind to use technology for enhanced quality of life. At this point in history, however, questions far outnumber enlightened responses.

With improved health care comes longer life expectancy. The inevitability of personal death thus slips into the background. Since death is not a pressing issue, neither is the ultimate goal of mortal life.

Because of greater opportunities for education, many of us are no longer willing to accept automatically much of what civil and ecclesial authorities hand down to us. We question, probe and challenge. We want to participate actively in the decisions which directly affect us. We have our own ideas and want to be free to form our own judgments. We wish to operate from an inner authority rather than merely live in conformity to rules and regulations.

(2) *Effects of Those Situations on the Experience of Vocation*

The above situations are for the most part indicative of progress. Yet, in this social context many Christians experience considerable confusion, uprooting and ambivalence in their faith. Vocation is a case in point. The presence of such spiritual unrest is itself neither good nor bad. It is a condition which accompanies change, especially constant change. It can be a catalyst for growth or an instrument of diminishment, depending on how the person and the community use it.

Many of us who reap the benefits from material and technological advancement allow this progress to be instrumental in our spiritual development. Yet, this positive involvement with creation produces a crisis of another kind. We realize that however valuable and spiritualizing human progress is, it can never totally satisfy us. Far from it! It causes us to discover within us an insatiable longing for something more—God.[3]

For communities to witness to vocation as an evangelical value, it is imperative that amid all the complexities of society we adults confront the mystery of calling in our personal lives. We have to wrestle with our own vocation before we can encourage emerging vocational consciousness in young community members. We need to discern carefully our own self-identity, lifestyle and mission before we can help others discern how God's calling, willing and caring affect their lives. Solitary prayer, study, spiritual direction and sharing in faith with fellow pilgrims assist this quest. With our own renewed sense of vocational awareness, we then become instrumental in the Lord's work of awakening others to their authentic callings.

B. Education

The Christian community, in fulfilling its responsibility for the vocational formation of its members, must also provide catechesis on the mystery of divine calling.

A first source of enlightenment for young Christians is the

[3]See *O Blessed Night*, 57–68; *Receptivity*, 17–31.

living faith of adults approaching life with the conviction of having been called by God. There is no substitute for youth actually seeing their spiritual guides practicing what they preach. The example that adults set usually has more far-reaching effects than anything they say.

The experience of a community being united in mind and heart amidst a diversity of callings is also a powerful influence upon Christian neophytes. This situation offers a variety of vocational models and possibilities which young persons can consider in awakening to their own calling. It attests to the fact that their community does not expect uniformity, but rather values the unique vocation of each person. The community's recognition of a diversity of callings encourages the aspiring Christian to be creative, to explore, to risk untrodden paths. Parents, especially, have to be aware that it is God who bestows a vocation upon their children, not the parents themselves. They may wish their children to become such-and-such, but they must never coerce them to do so.

To facilitate the emergence of vocational consciousness and commitment the Christian community needs also to present to its members a renewed theology of vocation. Parents and teachers must incorporate the theme of God's calling throughout the entire catechetical program. Instruction for all members—from the very young to the very mature—is necessary.

In the catechetical curriculum, spiritual leaders could present the theme of vocation in units designed according to the developmental stages of psychological and spiritual growth.[4] Thus, a person at each new phase of development would reconsider the mystery of vocation in accordance with his/her level of maturation.

Vocational catechesis is vital, for at stake is nothing less than the Christian sense of meaning and purpose in life.

C. Discernment

Providing competent spiritual direction to those discerning their vocation is a further responsibility of the Christian commu-

---

[4]See above "Chapter 11. Developmental Patterns of Vocational Consciousness" and our book *The Spiritual Journey*.

nity. Parents, teachers and mentors all have significant roles in furnishing this guidance. A spiritual director-directee relationship can be of invaluable assistance, especially when the Christian begins to rethink vocation in the context of personal relationship with God and with significant others.[5]

With respect to this vocational discernment, we highlight some specific responsibilities of spiritual guides:

(1) In order to establish a foundation for the discernment process, spiritual guides must help neophytes to formulate the proper questions. For instance, "How is the Lord calling me to serve God and God's people?" rather than "In which profession can I earn the most money and attain the greatest prestige?" Or again, "Through which combination of lifestyles can I best become the person God is calling me to be?" rather than "What way of life will offer me the most comfort and security with the least effort?"

(2) Spiritual guides must listen to God within those discerning their vocations. When appropriate, they can offer observations and suggestions. Most importantly, however, they need to witness a loving presence and a basic faith-seeking-understanding to these young Christians. That way, discernment will unfold in an atmosphere of trust and security.

(3) Spiritual guides have to be able to explain the basic principles of vocational discernment to those awakening to their calling. There are specific principles for discerning vocations to each Christian lifestyle and ministry. These guidelines, signs and conditions indicate authenticity or lack of it.

(4) When lifelong commitment is at issue, we cannot over-emphasize the importance of encouraging young Christians to wait out the process of emerging vocational consciousness. Not until they come to experience their personal calling as an existential inability to be, become or do otherwise are they ready to permanently commit themselves.

(5) Vocations—ministries especially—while bestowed by the Lord are called forth by the community. This commissioning can be effected by the Christian community at large, by the institutional Church or one's religious congregation, by the local com-

[5]See *Spiritual Direction*, 51–118.

munity, by one's spiritual director, pastor or minister. God interacts not only with the individual but also with the community in order to elicit vocational consciousness and to authenticate a calling.

(6) When a Christian does come to a basic sense of vocation and a readiness for permanent commitment to God through a Christian lifestyle, a final sign of the authenticity of that direction is affirmation from the community. A principal means of that affirmation is the celebration through meaningful rites of commitment of what God has brought forth in their midst.

D. Emancipation

The Christian who experiences God's calling as an existential inability is spiritually an adult. Thus, transformation of the relationship between the individual and the community accompanies mature vocational consciousness and commitment.

Up to the experience of an existential inability, that relationship is to a large extent parent-child. The person remains in a somewhat dependent position vis-à-vis the community. S/he seeks guidance, wisdom and nurturing from it, as a maturing child or adolescent does from a parent. When the person reaches mature vocational awareness, however, that individual is ready to relate to the community on an adult-adult basis. The committed Christian begins to value independence, collegiality, personal responsibility and mutual accountability vis-à-vis the Christian community.

Moreover, the person is ready to begin exercising spiritual leadership. S/he has the capacity to be an instrument of spiritual regeneration for others. As that individual's faith in Christ continues to evolve, the prophetic dimension of his/her vocation will become increasingly accentuated. Through that person, God will in some manner call the community itself beyond its current level of faith, hope and love.

In a way, this situation is an acid test of how Christianly mature a community is. The change in relationship from parent-child to adult-adult invites the community to gracefully relinquish a certain kind of control and power. The community as parent must decrease so that Christ in the emancipated member can increase all the more (John 3:30). That stance requires letting go the familiar for what is as yet untried and untested.

This transition from parent-child to adult-adult becomes especially difficult when a member moves ahead of the community's overall level of spiritual development. Instead of the community celebrating the spiritual emancipation of its member, some respond by mistrusting retreat or fearful denial. They may even persecute the emancipated person for being prophetic.

When the Christian community and an individual member welcome the transformation of their relationship and negotiate their way through the difficulties, both are enriched. They grow in unity amid diversity and bear witness to the unity and diversity of Father, Son and Spirit. This prayer of Jesus will then find greater fulfillment in their hearts and lives:

> Father, may they all be one,
>   as you are in me and as I am in you . . .
> With me in them and you in me,
>   may they be so completely one
>   that the world will recognize that you sent me and
>   that I have loved them as you have loved me
>   (John 17:21-23).

CHAPTER 15

The Sound of Gentle Silence

In this study of the development of vocational consciousness and commitment, we have focused primarily on the process leading up to the experience of vocation as an existential inability to be, become and do other than what God's calling impels us. Development, however, does not end at that point. Having attained mature vocational awareness and possibly having also embarked upon a lifelong commitment, where do we go from there?

Experience teaches that much development still lies ahead. Further maturation of vocational consciousness occurs as we pass through each of the critical thresholds and stages of transforming union and dark night. Ultimately, evolving vocational awareness and commitment bring us to the gentle silence of God, to being contemplative in God's loving embrace.

A. The General Movement

Two broad consecutive phases characterize our spiritual journey: first, that of developing ourselves and our world for Christ; and second, that of dying to ourselves and this world in loving abandonment to him. Those two phases of a single though complex movement encompass our immersion in creation for Christ and our emergence through creation with him.[1]

By immersing ourselves in creation, we participate directly in this dynamic: We increase so that Christ can increase in us and

[1] See *Spiritual Journey,* 45–50.

all around us. By emergence through creation, the same movement takes another direction: We decrease so that Christ can further increase in us and in our world (John 3:30). This rhythm of
the incarnation and of the paschal mystery is like breathing in
and breathing out, like the arsis and thesis of a musical measure.

In the phase of Emergence, the need to establish self-identity
and to contribute to the world gives way to the need to die to self
and the world. Having forged a vigorous self, we are now impelled to surrender it to the Lord. This diminishment is paradoxically also growth. In it and through it, we continue becoming
who God calls us to be—no longer primarily through actively
building ourselves up but rather through dying to self:

> The one who loses his/her life for my sake
>   will find it (Matt 10:39).
> Unless the seed falls into the ground and dies,
>   it remains only a single grain (John 12:24).

Ordinarily, in the context of developing ourselves and our
world for Christ, we come to experience God's calling as an existential inability. As we foster intimacy and friendship with Jesus,
together with the Father and the Spirit, God reveals to us the vocational lifestyle expressive of our personhood. That vocational
awareness is a firstfruit of immersion in creation for Christ. It initiates readiness for lifelong commitment.

After we experience God's call as residing within us, our vocational consciousness and commitment continue to unfold for
a time in the context of Immersion. Eventually, however, that
context changes radically. Our vocational awareness and our
commitment to God henceforth evolve in the context of
Emergence.

Besides being a general spiritual direction, Emergence denotes the critical threshold and the stage of adult spiritual genesis wherein we become explicitly aware of our need to surrender
ourselves to God. Moreover, as developing Christian adults we
experience other critical thresholds along the way: Personal
Conversion, Spiritual Espousal, Spiritual Marriage and Personal
Death/Resurrection.[2]

---

[2]See Ibid., 48.

While Emergence is in one sense a process culminating in death, Personal Conversion is a unique moment of breakthrough and stabilization in that process. In it, we irrevocably surrender ourselves in faith, hope and love to God. In Spiritual Espousal, we and Jesus abandon ourselves to each other as do intimate lovers. This deeper intimacy with Christ causes intense longing for the fullness of God. In Spiritual Marriage, God and the soul become one in transforming union insofar as it is possible in this life. The whole process is consummated in Personal Death/Resurrection.

Thus, the following questions arise: Along what lines do our vocational consciousness and commitment evolve as we emerge through creation? As we advance through those critical thresholds and stages of adult spiritual genesis, how do we experience vocational awareness and response? How might we describe the effects which deepening transformation in God have upon vocational consciousness and commitment?

B. Further Development: Reaffirmation and Recommitment

The First Book of Kings (19:9-14) uses powerful imagery to portray Elijah's encounter with God on Mount Horeb. We apply the dynamics of that encounter to the evolution of vocational consciousness and commitment in the course of our emergence through creation with Christ.

According to the story, Elijah walked forty days and forty nights until he reached the mountain of God. There he went into a cave and spent the night. The word of Yahweh came to him:

> What are you doing here, Elijah?
> To which he replied:
>   I am burning with zeal for Yahweh Sabaoth (vv. 9-10).

After explaining the circumstances which brought him to Horeb in the first place, the prophet was instructed to leave the cave and to stand on the mountain in the presence of God:

> A mighty wind arose splitting the mountains apart . . .
>   but Yahweh was not in the wind.
> After the wind, an earthquake erupted,

but Yahweh was not in the earthquake.
After the earthquake, a fire blazed forth,
but Yahweh was not in the fire.
And after the fire,
came the sound of gentle silence[3] (vv. 11-12).

At this point, a voice came to him a second time:

What are you doing here, Elijah?
To which he replied:
I am burning with zeal for Yahweh Sabaoth (vv. 13-14).

As the text stands, God twice asked Elijah the question: "What are you doing here?" (1 Kgs 19:9, 13). And the prophet twice responded with the identical words: "I am burning with zeal for Yahweh Sabaoth" (1 Kgs 19:10, 14). The two questions and responses are separated by the experience of wind, earthquake, fire and silence. What might this repeated question and response symbolize? In the first instance, the prophet was in his own way affirming who he understood himself to be and what he saw as the direction of his life. He was proclaiming his commitment to the Lord. In the second instance, Elijah was in his own way re-affirming who he understood himself to be and what he saw as the direction of his life. He was re-committing himself to Yahweh.

Our vocational reaffirmation and recommitment occur in a manner similar to that of Elijah.

Throughout the stage of Immersion we ask the Lord to reveal to us who we are, how God wills us to live, what God wants us to do. We seek in various ways to discover meaning and purpose in life. We collaborate with God in the work of both self-development and the development of our world. The experience of vocation as an existential inability to be, become and do otherwise brings us to a basic resolution of those issues. When we arrive at that resolution, however, the tables are turned. No sooner do we reach the threshold of a mature sense of voca-

---

[3]Literally, the Hebrew text reads "a sound of finely ground silence." The verb "to grind finely" evokes the image of wheat being pulverized by a mill. More poetic translations render the phrase: the sound of fragile stillness, the thunder of delicate silence, a still small voice, the whispering of gentle air, the sound of a rustling breeze.

tional direction than the Lord poses to us the very questions we had been asking of God. The Lord inquires: "What are you all about now? What is your deeper purpose in life? Where are you really from and where are you ultimately heading?" Thus, as soon as we attain mature vocational affirmation and commitment, God invites us to reaffirm and to recommit ourselves, our lifestyle and our mission.

Elijah's initial affirmation of his vocation and commitment to Yahweh established the foundation for his eventual reaffirmation and recommitment. Moreover, this rededication marked a fuller participation in the direction in which the Lord had been already leading him. The prophet's first commitment thus readied him for deeper intimacy with God. This more intimate communion was, however, entirely at the Lord's initiative. What Elijah had to do was wait—wait in that desert of the heart—until God had prepared him interiorly to respond to his maturing vocation.

The experience of God's calling as an existential inability sets us on solid vocational ground. The within and the without of our lives harmonize. We have an integrated and integrating prayer life.[4] Synchronicity exists in relation to the three basic facets of vocation: self-identity, lifestyle and mission. Yet, that vocational consciousness is also the catalyst which sets us in the direction of a deeper surrender to God. That vocational awareness impels us toward God through dying more voluntarily to self and through experiencing acute aridity in our lifestyle and mission.[5] Maturing vocational awareness sets us on the course of night, of desert, of the Cross. There we have to let the Lord exert the initiative while we let God be done in us. As God further intensifies vocational awareness, our fundamental stance is that of increasingly loving receptivity.

C. Further Development: The Spiritual Journey

While standing in Yahweh's presence, Elijah found that the more intimately he encountered God, the more he became detached and uprooted from all that was familiar and secure. This

---

[4]See *Contemplation*, 125–140.
[5]See Ibid., 60–71; *Spiritual Journey*, 99–113.

dynamic is evident in his experience of the mighty wind, the earthquake and the fire. These are symbols of progressively more powerful, awesome and purifying encounters with the Lord.

The wind, like a hurricane, tore up boulders and shattered rock. This signifies that Elijah had to let go many things which up to that time he had valued and esteemed. The earthquake caused the ground to crumble beneath his feet. Thus, the foundations of his faith and the meaning of his life were shaken. He had to let go his basic security. Then came the fire—the most purifying of all. It cleansed and healed as if by cauterization.

The text, however, insists that Yahweh was not in the wind, the earthquake or the fire. Typical of the Semitic mind, this suggests that while Elijah experienced something of God on each occasion, he did not encounter the Lord directly. Yahweh is more than those experiences could reveal. That "more"—the inner life of God—is symbolized by the "sound of gentle silence."

The deepening of our vocational consciousness and commitment from the critical threshold of Emergence onward is comparable to Elijah's experience of God on Mount Horeb.

As we traverse Emergence, Personal Conversion, Spiritual Espousal and Spiritual Marriage, a pattern recurs in each instance. Intimate encounter with God at each of these critical thresholds of adult spiritual genesis uproots us from all that is familiar. In the context of dying ever more deeply to self for Christ, our passage through each stage elicits questioning and reevaluation of our self-identity, lifestyle and mission. Therefore, implicit to each critical threshold of adult spiritual development is a vocational crisis.

(1) *Emergence through Creation: A Mighty Wind*

Entering the threshold and the stage of Emergence is like being struck by a hurricane. Having experienced vocation as an existential inability to be, become or do otherwise, we burn with enthusiasm to be faithful to God's calling. We feel peace, joy and security. Then, when we least expect it, some horrendous force strikes. It uproots everything we had grown accustomed to and whisks away all we so treasured.

Regarding involvement with creation, an all-pervasive aridity overtakes our gusto. At times, we fear spiritual bankruptcy. Anxiety and restlessness besiege us. We find ourselves questioning and rethinking every aspect of life. A need to be alone more frequently with God in silence creeps upon us.[6]

This shift in direction arises from the fact that God has begun to commune with us in a transformed manner. Previously, the Lord communicated with us principally through media such as feelings, symbols, thoughts and gestures. Now God interacts with us in an increasingly immediate and direct way. The Spirit leads us beyond the perceptible into mystery, beyond the sensory to the spiritual, beyond security and certitude to deeper faith, hope and love.

(2) *Personal Conversion: An Earthquake*

Vocationally, the critical threshold of Personal Conversion is like Elijah's experience of the earthquake.[7] It occurs when we have hit rock-bottom, when the very ground we stand on breaks apart. We have to make an earth-shattering choice between God and self-centeredness, growth and self-destruction, forward movement or regression into isolation. Turning so radically toward God means also irrevocably reaffirming our vocation in life.

(3) *The Dark Night of Spirit: A Consuming Fire*

In preparation for the critical threshold of Spiritual Espousal, we undergo fire. The Lord's burning love transforms and purifies our spirit. It cauterizes our most hidden depths. Thus, it transforms us more and more in God, and consumes in us all that is un-God-like.[8]

(4) *Spiritual Espousal and Spiritual Marriage: The Sound of Gentle Silence*

The grace of Spiritual Espousal can be compared to Elijah's encounter with Yahweh in the sound of gentle silence.[9] Prior to

---

[6]See *Spiritual Journey*, 102–113; *Contemplation*, 53–75.
[7]See *Spiritual Journey*, 135–162.
[8]See Ibid., 163–198.
[9]See Ibid., 201–211.

this threshold, we were mainly conscious of the purifying or consuming aspect of God's love. The night was dark indeed. In this betrothal, however, the accent shifts. The transforming dimension of divine love asserts itself more forcefully upon our consciousness. We, nonetheless, continue to experience the night, but in this context as tranquil.

Throughout Spiritual Espousal and Spiritual Marriage,[10] the reevaluation and reaffirmation of our vocational commitment occur increasingly in the light of transforming love. Awareness of being-in-love with God directly shapes our consciousness of our self-identity, lifestyle and mission. Moreover, we become progressively inclined to view our entire vocation as an invitation to love and to be loved.

> Who am I called to be?
>   To be fully myself, transformed in love by God.
> How am I called to become myself?
>   By love.
> What am I called to do in the process of this becoming?
>   To love.

St. Thérèse of the Child Jesus bears outstanding witness to that truth. She felt within herself many vocational longings—to be a priest, an apostle, a doctor of the Church, a martyr, a Carmelite, etc. Yet, she experienced all those callings eventually converge on one—love:

> Love gave me the key to my vocation. . . . I came to understand that the Church had a Heart and that this Heart was burning with love. . . . I could see that love comprised all vocations, that love was everything, that it embraced all times and places . . . in a word, that it was eternal. Then, overwhelmed with joy, I exclaimed: O Jesus, my Love. . . . At last I have discovered my calling. . . . *My vocation is love!*. . . . In the heart of the Church, I shall be *love*. Thus, I shall be everything and my yearning will be fulfilled.[11]

[10]See Ibid., 212–222.
[11]See St. Thérèse of the Child Jesus, *Story of a Soul: The Autobiography of St. Therese of Lisieux*, trans. John Clarke (Washington, D.C.: Institute of Carmelite Studies Publications, 1972) 193–194.

(5) *Death/Resurrection: Transformed in God by God*

Our Personal Death/Resurrection marks the culmination of our vocational convergence on divine love.[12] Transformed in Love, by Love, we remain for all eternity in love with our Beloved and loving all creation in Father, Son and Spirit.

As we pass through Emergence, Personal Conversion, Spiritual Espousal, Spiritual Marriage and Personal Death/Resurrection, we experience in each critical threshold a radical increase of self-knowledge, consciousness and freedom. Consequently, we have also at each successive threshold increased capacity to opt for God and to commune more intensely with God in faith, hope and love. We are thus able to experience our evolving self-identity, lifestyle and mission from an ever greater depth of personhood. Finally, in our death/resurrection we commit ourselves with all our heart to our Beloved. As we die to ourselves and to this mortal existence, we ever more freely and voluntarily accept the fullness of God's calling.

D. Being Contemplative in God's Loving Embrace

After Elijah had undergone the mighty wind, the earthquake, the fire and the sound of gentle silence, Yahweh again asked him: "What are you doing here?" (1 Kgs 19:13). Astonishingly, after so much transformation and purification, the prophet responded exactly as he had before: "I am burning with zeal for Yahweh Sabaoth." (1 Kgs 19:14). Elijah could find no better way to verbalize his experience of vocational consciousness. Yet, that recommitment surely emanated from a immeasurably deeper sense of mystery, self-awareness and freedom.

Our evolving vocational consciousness and commitment, after the experience of God's calling as an existential inability, have many similarities to Elijah's second response to the Lord.

On the one hand, like the prophet most of us have a long story to tell. Our winding, multifaceted spiritual journey comprises several lifestyles and many ministries over the course of time. God's calling may have even required that at some point

---

[12]See *Spiritual Journey*, 223–226.

we engage in radical vocational changes. There are many callings within our personal call to holiness.

On the other hand, also like Elijah, the more we mature spiritually, the less we can say about God's calling. In our vocational development, the Lord increasingly brings to light our illusions, limitations and sinfulness; our addictions, codependencies and attachments. We see how complex our motivations were in originally committing ourselves to God through a particular lifestyle or ministry. Along with a degree of sincerity, we discover many other influences upon our decision-making: selfishness, woundedness, misguided choices, hidden agendas, etc. Yet, we realize that God incorporated all that inner poverty into the formation of our vocation. The gentle silence of the Lord enlightens us with truth. That truth in turn reduces us to silence before Yahweh. It leaves us contemplative in God's loving embrace.

Silence invites silence. Deep calls unto deep. Love begets love. Such is our vocation and our awareness of it.

Because God's calling lies at the core of what is most mysterious and ineffable in our personhood, we can never in this life totally grasp, fathom or complete a Christian vocation. God actualizes it painstakingly. We discover it gradually. We reaffirm and recommit ourselves to the Lord through it over and over again. God's calling reaches its consummation in our personal death/resurrection. Yet, the more deeply we encounter God dwelling within us, the greater our freedom to receive the ontological, moral and spiritual imperatives which that calling effects within us. Thus, we abide ever more deeply in the mystery proclaimed by Jesus:

> You did not choose me.
> No, I chose you,
>> and I have sent you forth to bear lasting fruit
>> (John 15:16).

CONCLUSION

Vocation as Mystery

Throughout this book, we have developed a theology of vocation and lifelong commitment from an evolutionary and relational point of view.

We say "evolutionary" for three principal reasons: (1) because our calling evolves from our inception to death, (2) our awareness of that evolving vocation progresses through various phases of development and (3) our response—especially in terms of commitment—intensifies as we mature.

We say "relational," because that growth takes place in intimate relationship and interaction with God, with people, with our maturing personhood and with the world around us.

We have approached Christian vocation above all from the perspective of mystery. We can never reduce divine calling to human processes or reasonable options, nor to mere feelings or personality traits. We cannot neatly package into categories or pigeonhole into prearranged slots God's way of transforming us. Every vocation pertains to the mystery of the Lord's inexhaustible love for an individual:

> Oh, the depths of the riches and of the wisdom of God!
> How inscrutable the Lord's judgments!
> How unsearchable God's ways! (Rom 11:33).

That mystery, however, resides not only in the Lord, but also in our inner poverty:

> Think of yourselves when you were called.

> Not many of you were wise by human standards,
>   or influential, or born into high society.
> God chose rather the foolish in the eyes of the world
>   to confound the wise. . . .
> God chose these who were lowly according to worldly standards
>   to shame those who think they are everything. . . .
> Therefore, let none of us boast before God
>   (1 Cor 1:26-29).

Yes, vocation remains profoundly a mystery.

What is mystery? Most of us would respond: It is a religious truth which we can know only by divine revelation, but which even when known cannot be fully understood. Or again: Mystery refers to a certain kind of knowledge, the attainment of which requires a special initiation.

In the context of vocation, "mystery" denotes both those responses and more. The word *mystérion* is found some twenty-seven times in the New Testament, mostly in Pauline writings.[1] The Letter to the Ephesians even speaks of marriage—one of the lifestyles which we treat—as a "great mystery" (Eph 5:32). As it relates to divine calling, *mystérion* accentuates three dimensions of God's interaction with us:

- mystery as the content of God's revelation,
- mystery as it underlies the unfolding of human history,
- mystery as pointing to the final consummation of creation, the eschaton.

(1) In the New Testament, mystery is presented as the content of revelation. The Lord makes known to us something of God's inner life as well as of the Lord's intimate dealings with us. Ultimately, "the mystery of God is Christ, in whom is hidden all the treasures of wisdom and knowledge" (Col 2:2-3).

Mystery relates to vocation in that we experience our calling as a manifestation of the Lord's formative and transformative activity within us and all around us. This vocational activity is both for us and for others. It is furthermore a mutual activity in several senses: We collaborate directly with God, and we work also with others who interact with us and with God.

[1] See *TDNT*, IV:802–828.

Whenever the Lord wills our voluntary cooperation in the unfolding of our mysterious vocation, God somehow reveals what we need to know. To awaken this awareness, the Lord employs a multitude of means, the most usual of which is discernment. Discernment has many faces in diverse contexts, but in most instances it moves forward within the confluence of faith, intuition and common sense.

(2) The mystery of God is the wisdom and the will of the Lord made manifest in space and time. That manifestation occurs not only on a cosmic scale, but also in a personal manner for each human being. The unfolding of our vocation is an especially significant way in which divine wisdom and the divine will embrace our individual salvation histories.

The development of that mystery occurs in dialogue with all the situations which comprise our day-to-day existence. These include every facet of our psychosocial and psychosexual growth, our emotional and physical maturation, our faith and consciousness development. Everything in the world around us and everything within us affect somehow the evolution of our calling.

(3) Whatever other meaning the word may have, each New Testament usage of *mystérion* contains an eschatological sense. The noun "mystery" always refers in one way or another to the final outcome of God's design, not only for the entire cosmos but also for every person.

Vocation as mystery, therefore, evokes the goal of all self-identity, each lifestyle and every ministry. That goal is transformation in God by God. The discovering and the voluntary living out of our vocation is at the very core of the process of transforming union, of deification, of divinization.

Sic fínis líbri, non aútem óperis.